WHEN
ADS
WORK

WHEN ADS WORK

NEW PROOF THAT ADVERTISING TRIGGERS SALES

SECOND EDITION

JOHN PHILIP JONES

M.E.Sharpe
Armonk, New York
London, England

Library of Congress Cataloging-in-Publication Data

Jones, John Philip.
When ads work : new proof that advertising triggers sales / by John Philip Jones.— 2nd ed.
  p. cm.
Includes bibliographical references and index.
ISBN-13: 978-0-7656-1738-5 (cloth : alk. paper) — ISBN-13: 978-0-7656-1739-2 (pbk. : alk. paper)
ISBN-10: 0-7656-1738-2 (cloth : alk. paper) — ISBN-10: 0-7656-1739-0 (pbk. : alk. paper)
  1. Advertising—Case studies. 2. Sales promotion—Case studies. I. Title.

HF5823.J719 2006
659.1—dc22   2006005852

Printed in the United States of America

The paper used in this publication meets the minimum requirements of
American National Standard for Information Sciences
Permanence of Paper for Printed Library Materials,
ANSI Z 39.48-1984.

⊗

EB (c) 10   9   8   7   6   5   4   3   2   1
EB (p) 10   9   8   7   6   5   4   3   2   1

To Dennis Tobolski, Patrick Kung, and Vincent Wong

Practical experience in itself is of little use unless
it forms the basis of reflection and thought.
—Bernard Law Montgomery

Contents

Tables and Figures

Tables

Figures

Preface

This book (like its first edition) is dedicated to three computer experts, Dennis Tobolski, Patrick Kung, and Vincent Wong. These are the people who made it possible for me to make sense of the rich and complex information on consumer buying and television viewing that had been collected for two years by A.C. Nielsen. They were therefore instrumental in giving me access to the data on which this book is based. Before I began to work on the Nielsen figures in 1993, I had a fairly clear idea of the type of analysis that was going to be needed, but I did not have the faintest idea how to generate and cluster the information in the way I wanted. The three people to whom the book is dedicated turned my vision of how the figures should be related to one another into the reality of robust statistical tables.

Four other people—all personal friends—also deserve mention because of their influence on this work. They are Timothy Joyce, Colin McDonald, Simon Broadbent, and Erwin Ephron. Erwin Ephron is the sole American in the company of three Britishers, in addition to myself (and I have dual nationality).

Timothy Joyce (who died in 1997) was intellectually the most remarkable market researcher I have ever known. He left Cambridge with a PhD in philosophy and did not enter the world of survey research until he was in his late twenties, when he joined the British Market Research Bureau (BMRB), the research arm of the London branch of the leading American advertising agency J. Walter Thompson (JWT). I had also worked at BMRB, and I spent most of my advertising career with J. Walter Thompson. At the beginning of his career, Timothy Joyce demonstrated his originality by attacking the key problem faced by people who want to find out how advertising works. He constructed a device that later became known as the advertising planning index (API), which collected aggregated data on the buying of brands and the amount of advertising for those same brands.

The API led directly to the now well-established American research systems run by the Simmons Market Research Bureau (SMRB) and Mediamark Research Inc. (MRI), both of which were also started by Timothy Joyce. These research services are today indispensable for all advertising media planners in the United States.

However, these systems fall short of the method of pure single-source research: the special and particularly expensive technique on which this book is based. However, in the early 1960s, Timothy Joyce had begun to think about how to apply this more rigorous and difficult method, and he managed to find the funds (from JWT London) to launch an experimental research program in 1966. (This test is described in Appendix B.) Timothy Joyce joined A.C. Nielsen in the United States during the early 1990s, and he called on me to develop the pure single-source technique on a broad scale, using A.C. Nielsen data. This was an enormous professional opportunity for me, and from the beginning I was fascinated by it.

The second person I must mention is Colin McDonald, who actually carried out this first experiment in pure single-source research at BMRB. This was a work of seminal importance that led to much debate and action, although—astonishingly—it was not replicated until my own much larger-scale work that was reported in the first edition of this book, published in 1995. This shows a delay of almost thirty years! Colin McDonald had studied "Greats" (i.e., the Greek and Roman classics and philosophy) at Oxford: a fact that demonstrates yet again the value of an education rooted in the humanities.

My third friend was Simon Broadbent, who was educated at *both* Oxford *and* Cambridge. He built his career at the Leo Burnett advertising agency in London and Chicago, and his work was concentrated essentially on advertising's longer-term effects. Simon Broadbent was the guru of advertising research in Britain. He was a widely published author and a very influential figure.

He and I disagreed about how we thought advertising works. I am totally convinced that advertising must generate an immediate jolt to sales before it can be expected to produce any further effect, and all the evidence in this book points to this fact. On the other hand, Simon Broadbent believed that advertising's effect is felt exclusively in the long term, and he developed an independent variable, which he called AdStock, to be used in econometric models. This is a figure that represents the lingering but decaying influence of each brand's advertising on its sales. He stimulated my own thinking about the long-term effects of advertising, and in 2002 I published a book on the subject based on broad-scale econometric data.[1] Simon Broadbent had earlier published a book titled *When to Advertise*,[2] in which he devoted a chapter substantially to my work. The first section of this chapter has the title "John Philip Jones and 'Once Is Enough.'" He reviewed my research fairly, but he disagreed with much of it. He and I were personally very close until his death in 2002.

My fourth friend and colleague, Erwin Ephron, will appear later in this preface.

When my work on pure single-source research had been completed, I made a number of presentations to audiences of research and advertising practitioners, and I began to publish papers in professional journals. With the first appearance of this book, there was a torrent of interest. Many respected figures in research and advertising in different countries made warm and occasionally flattering comments. I do not wish to belabor the degree of support I received, but I was particularly gratified to hear the following comment from Michael Naples, at the time president of the Advertising Research Foundation, an independent body funded by the largest organizations in the advertising industry. It is by far the leading advertising research organization in the world, and it publishes the *Journal of Advertising Research*, the preeminent publication in its field. This is what Naples said:

> In this book, Jones continues the important work he began in 1986 with the publication of *What's in a Name?* His new book remarkably extends his data-intensive examination of advertising's productivity, and in the process turns what others have viewed as data overload into a Single-Source data mother lode. Astonishingly, he succeeds in putting advertising exposure effects under a microscope every bit as powerful as that which the original UPC Code Scanner Data did for short-term promotion measurement. His accomplishment is one to which no one else has yet been able to lay claim.[3]

However, as a corrective, I am equally proud of a letter I received from David Ogilvy, who during the latter part of the twentieth century was the most respected advertising figure in the world. His brief and charming letter to me made it perfectly clear that he was totally unable to understand anything I had written in the book! This letter is reproduced in facsimile at the end of Chapter 6.

Two important research-related developments took place following the first edition of *When Ads Work*. The first was that the research was replicated in Japan and at least five countries in Europe. This multinational research confirmed my original findings to a most striking degree. (See Chapter 3.) *When Ads Work* had high sales for such a specialist work, and it sold in all English-speaking markets. Special editions were also published, translated into Spanish, Portuguese, Japanese, Chinese, Korean, Arabic, and Turkish.

The second thing that happened was the direct result of a key finding of my research. This was that advertising, if it is creatively effective, generates sales from a *single exposure*, and if the advertiser runs the advertising more often than once during the few days before the brand is bought, these incremental exposures work with sharply declining efficiency. It follows from this important insight that it is uneconomic to pile up advertising pressure in the few days before purchasing takes place. This had been precisely the strategy of most advertisers before the lessons of *When Ads Work* began to sink in. The research that is directly relevant to media planning appears in Chapter 5.

This firm evidence was used by Erwin Ephron, the fourth of my friends, when he developed and began to propagate the theory of continuity planning, a clearly articulated doctrine that recommends reducing the level of media concentration below what used to be considered necessary, and redeploying the money saved by stretching it over more weeks of the year.

It is not an exaggeration to say that continuity planning has revolutionized media strategy in the United States and in many other countries. It is a policy now applied by most major advertisers. And there is good evidence from many case studies that it is more cost-efficient than any strategy of concentrated media pressure. (Some of these cases are described in Chapter 5.) Continuity planning has led to a change in the pattern of media spending for advertisers whose combined budgets can be measured in billions of dollars. This change was the direct result of the vision and energy of Erwin Ephron and the way he managed to exploit the supporting evidence that I had supplied and that was first published in *When Ads Work.*

In the first edition, I expressed thanks to a number of other friends for their valuable contributions when they reviewed the text. I repeat their names here: the late Leo Bogart, Richard Burton, Steve Coffey, Andrew Ehrenburg, Kelly Forrest, Michael Naples, Andrew Tarshis, and the late William Weilbacher.

Finally, I reserve my most profound thanks to my wife, Wendy. With both editions of this book, she transformed my scrappy writing and constant corrections into impeccable manuscripts with her usual skill, meticulous care, and a most remarkable degree of patience.

This second edition of *When Ads Work* is structured in the same way as the first edition, but there has been a good deal of change in the text.

Part I: Facts Replace Theory. This first part of the book has been substantially rewritten in order to clarify my description of the data and to incorporate the findings of the many pieces of research using the same technique that have been published since the 1st Edition came out. Part 1 in the second edition is longer than in the first edition.

Part II: Evidence for Part I: Seventy-Eight Brands Dissected. This part of the book clusters the brands I researched into four groups, named Alpha One, Alpha Two, Beta, and Gamma. The selection was based on the relative effectiveness of each brand's advertising. This part is substantially unchanged from the first edition, although it has been slightly shortened.

Appendixes. One appendix has been omitted in the second edition. But the remaining five appendixes are unchanged. These are an important part of the book, and I advise readers to study them carefully.

Notes

1. John Philip Jones, *The Ultimate Secrets of Advertising* (Thousand Oaks, CA: Sage Publications, 2002).

2. Simon Broadbent, *When to Advertise* (Henley-on-Thames, UK: Admap Publications, in association with the Incorporated Society of British Advertisers and the Institute of Practitioners in Advertising, 1999).

3. This quotation appears on the dust jacket of the first edition of *When Ads Work.*

I

Facts Replace Theory

1

The Single-Source Breakthrough

This book is concerned exclusively with sales and how advertising influences them. To make this point more precisely, I believe that advertising works only when it influences consumer purchasing behavior. This does not mean only that nonbuyers must be persuaded to become first-time buyers, nor that current buyers should be persuaded to buy more of the brand than before. On the contrary, advertising can sometimes be effective if it helps maintain a brand's existing users and their buying levels. This is known technically as protecting the brand's franchise and keeping up the current levels of purchase frequency. Advertising can even work if sales are going down as a result of competitive pressure on the brand in the market place, because effective advertising may be helping to slow this process. Finally, a behavioral effect can be felt if buyers are persuaded to pay a premium price for an advertised brand, even though sales in units may not necessarily be increasing.

There is a large and well-established research industry engaged in measuring the psychological impact of advertising campaigns: their effect on brand awareness, image attributes, and advertising recall—that is, whether consumers can remember the brand name, what qualities they associate with the brand, and what features of the brand's advertising have remained in their minds. These measures are most commonly used as substitutes for sales measures in the widespread belief that it is too difficult to measure reliably advertising's contribution to sales. I do

3

not accept these counsels of despair. Psychological measures are very poor predictors of sales effectiveness, for reasons that I spelled out in a book first published in 1986.[1] Psychological measures can, however, help us diagnose how a campaign is working once we have determined from more reliable research that it is in fact working. But that is a different story altogether.

Advertising That Works

Advertising that works in the short term is defined here as advertising that is seen by a consumer shortly before he (or more commonly she—the female homemaker) purchases a brand and that influences the consumer's choice of that brand. The total number of consumers so influenced and the volume of merchandise purchased should be quantifiable. This is a difficult procedure, but it is not a totally impenetrable problem when tackled with the use of single-source data—the special type of research on which this book is based. In my analyses, I make the assumption that the time period during which the effective (or ineffective) advertising is exposed is seven days prior to purchase. The short-term effect of advertising is therefore brand advertising and brand buying within an average purchase interval: the period between the homemaker's last purchase and the next one in the product field.

The actual purchase interval varies between product categories. It is every few days (sometimes even daily) for cigarettes, every week for certain food products (e.g., breakfast cereals), every two to four weeks for other grocery products (e.g., mayonnaise) and some drugstore products (e.g., toothpaste), and every few months for many drugstore products (e.g., analgesics). With goods that have short purchase intervals, I have taken seven days as a reasonable approximation of their average buying interval. With the products that have a relatively extended purchase interval, I have also assumed that a short-term effect measures something felt and acted on also within a seven-day period. There is good evidence that short-term advertising effects are felt within this seven-day window. (This evidence is described in Appendix B.)

In addition to its short-term effect, advertising can often also have a longer-term effect. This book covers the medium-term effect of advertising, felt over the course of a year. In the analyses of the medium term I measure a brand's average sales over the second, third, and fourth quarters of 1991 and compare them with sales in the first quarter. My definition of medium term is therefore a four- to twelve-month period (compared with one week for a short-term effect).

Advertising's influence can normally also be felt over a longer time than the four to twelve months used in this book. A brand's internal momentum can operate and grow in effectiveness over very extended periods.[2] In this book, however, the medium-term effect of advertising is manifested in the four- to twelve-month span. The advantage of looking at a period of twelve months is that it provides the decision point at which all parts of a brand's marketing mix are usually evaluated.

My fifty years of experience in the advertising business have taught me that the impact of effective advertising on sales is more immediate than many observers think.[3] I therefore believe that the periods used in this book to define the short and medium term are the best alternatives.

The Meaning of Single-Source Research

This book is based on single-source research generated by the A.C. Nielsen Company. Many people responsible for brands are uncomfortable with certain types of quantitative research, because the research industry has tended not to be user-friendly. However, single-source research—despite its cost and the complications involved in implementing it—is in essence a simple technique, and its findings are easy to understand.

Single-source is not new. However, the pure method used by Nielsen is so unusual as to be almost unique. It is greatly more valuable—but also much more difficult to employ—than the diluted method, which will also be described and which has been used fairly widely over the course of the last thirty years.

Market research is carried out in three phases. Surveys are planned, fieldwork is carried out, and the data are analyzed. Information is collected in two ways: first by monitoring, observing, or picking up data mechanically (e.g., with scanners and other types of electronic meters), and second by asking people (e.g., buyers of a product category) to provide information and opinions. The market research industry is split approximately evenly between the two systems.[4] Advertising effects can be evaluated reliably only with the use of monitoring devices. The intervention of consumers introduces many inaccuracies and too many pieces of inexact data to produce robust conclusions.

Sales of a brand depend on many market place variables. The most important of these are consumer satisfaction with the functional properties of the brand in comparison with its competitors; the advertising, as the source of the brand's added values; the price, which is mainly expressed through its trade and consumer promotions; the brand's distribution and display in the retail trade; market place parameters, notably seasonality; and—a very important factor—the activities of competitive brands.

The major difficulty we find when evaluating the influence of advertising is determining how to isolate it. How do we untangle advertising's effect from all the other factors impinging on sales? And even if we manage to establish a clear relationship between advertising and sales, for instance between exposure of households to a brand's advertising (based on a large statistical sample of such households) and sales of the brand measured from another large group, how do we know that there is a direct cause-and-effect relationship between the two?

There is a well-known trap for the unwary. It is widely understood that in many important product categories, such as breakfast cereals, high levels of television viewing by buyers of Brand A are often associated statistically with high sales of Brand A, but high levels of television viewing by buyers of Brand B and Brand C are also often associated statistically with high sales of Brand A. It turns out that there is not much of a cause-and-effect relationship between the television viewing of advertising by buyers of Brand A and sales of Brand A. The real reason for this sales pattern is that both phenomena stem from a common cause—the presence of children in the household. More television is watched because of the children, leading to greater exposure to advertising for Brands A, B, and C, and more products are consumed because households with children are generally larger than average size.[5] Unless we subject the statistics to a very rigorous analysis or unless we look *at each individual household* (which we do with single-source research), we shall continue to be confused by such spurious relationships.

One way the market research industry has met the challenge of such statistical confusion is by borrowing a tough mathematical technique from the econometricians, who use it for the analysis of microeconomic and macroeconomic data. This technique takes statistics from separate and unconnected sources, for example, consumer panel or retail audit figures measuring the sales of different brands, estimates (from different auditing organizations) of the advertising budgets and the patterns of media expenditure for those brands, and a number of other measures. The different data sets are compared and analyzed. Taking the sales of a selected brand as the end result (known technically as the dependent variable), all the other sets of information are analyzed to determine the relative importance of each of them as causes (described technically as independent variables). This is done by the statistical device of multivariate regression, and it is often possible at the end of the calculations to construct a mathematical model that quantifies the relative importance of each of the individual influences on the sales of the brand. The role of advertising can be isolated in this way, and as a part of this process it is possible to calculate a brand's advertising elasticity; that is, the percentage by which the sales of the brand are likely to increase as the result of a 1 percent increase in advertising expenditure alone.

This type of analysis has great practical value and has been carried out on hundreds of occasions. It is very complicated, however. It requires mathematical skills of the highest order. Line managers—the very people who should be using the information—are often unable to understand it. And a model is occasionally incomplete, since it can fail to explain the compete picture of a brand's sales because of missing elements that the model cannot detect.

An alternative system to multivariate regression is controlled experimentation in the market place. Two (or more) regions are selected, and the brand is marketed in an identical way in each region except for variations in the advertising such as changes in copy, in the amount of media money spent, or in patterns of media exposure. Controlled experiments of this type have been run extensively, but they are generally very expensive to implement, take a lot of time, and are difficult to monitor. They also often yield fuzzy and indeterminate results because the differences between the areas are often greater than the differences between the specific advertising variables being tested.

In Britain, a technique known as the area marketing test evaluation system (AMTES), which combines regional testing with econometric evaluation, was developed by Beecham (now Glaxo Smith Kline) and has been used successfully for a number of years. AMTES has not been employed much in the United States. Its lack of popularity here has been difficult to understand, but may be due to suspicion of any techniques developed in foreign countries (something I have observed over many years)!

The general fault of the econometric systems is their mathematical complexity, the inevitable consequence of the way in which they attempt to describe a complex world. The problem with market place experimentation is expense, plus the practical impediments to finding comparable regions. In the face of these difficulties, the ingenuity of market researchers eventually succeeded in producing a third system that is both original and simple and which holds the promise of replacing both econometrics and market experimentation as a device for measuring accurately advertising's contribution to sales.

This was the genesis of single-source research. The technique focuses attention on the fieldwork stage rather than the analytical stage, and it does this at the very beginning of the research by bringing together the data that must be compared to establish statistical relationships.

With single-source research, the information is collected at the same time from the same people. It brings together a household's exposure to marketing stimuli (e.g., a brand's advertising) and purchases of that brand within the same household. An experienced marketing practitioner has described this method as the missing link to consumer product research.

Single-source is, however, a description that has come to be interpreted imprecisely. It is now generally seen as research that can be carried out in a number of different ways and with varying degrees of rigor. In particular, the phrase "a household's exposure to marketing stimuli (e.g., a brand's advertising)" is capable of more than one meaning.

At the looser extreme, household exposure to advertising can be measured in a simple way by looking at consumer purchasing of identified brands and at these consumers' overall exposure to specific media. This is the type of information provided by Mediamark Research Inc. (MRI) and Simmons Market Research Bureau (SMRB) and used for media targeting. It represents a significant step beyond relying on demographics. At the looser end, also, are the types of single-source research that concentrate on area testing: a system by which variations in the amounts of a brand's advertising received by consumers in different regions are related to those same consumers' purchases of the brand. In this book I name systems like these *diluted single-source research.*

They are different from the method employed when the system was first explored. This exploration took place in the United Kingdom in 1966, and the person most associated with the work was Colin McDonald. (McDonald's study is described in detail in Appendix B.) I call McDonald's original system *pure single-source research.* Pure single-source research determines each household's reception of advertising for specific identified brands and relates this to the purchasing of those same brands by the same household shortly after the advertising.

Most single-source research (pure and diluted) captures the short-term sales effect of advertising. It does this by focusing on the individual household. The data-collection system is described technically as disaggregated, and from this disaggregated foundation—from this large collection of statistical observations, or little bits of knowledge each relating to separate homes—the figures can be clustered (or aggregated) to throw light on the variables in which we are interested. In its ability to isolate one variable while all the others remain constant, single-source research bears some resemblance to market place experimentation: a long-established and (despite its problems) often respected technique.

Remember that with single-source research, the different types of data are collected together within the same household. We do not need to relate the various data sets to one another after the event, at the analysis stage (as with multivariate regression), because this has already taken place at the fieldwork stage. The clusters of statistical observations simply have to be assembled in a common-sense way to throw light on the problem being examined—for example, is there any difference between the purchasing of a brand by those households that receive advertisements for it and by the households that do not?

As mentioned, the first use of pure single-source research was by Colin McDonald in the United Kingdom in 1966. During the 1970s and 1980s, new types of single-source research were introduced, the meaning of single-source underwent some mutations, and the concept itself became diluted. The proceedings of various conferences sponsored by the Advertising Research Foundation and devoted to this type of research use at least fourteen separate definitions, all different from that given in this chapter.[6]

During the 1980s, single-source research began to lose its focus on advertising and therefore its unique advantage: its ability to measure advertising effects. It became increasingly associated with scanner data collected at the checkout of food stores. The term also came to mean data relating to a substantial number of variables. Indeed advertising descended in importance as promotional actions of different types began to take more prominent places in data collection (reflecting the fact that sales promotions were beginning to account for a larger share of advertising-plus-promotional budgets than advertising itself). These developments are reviewed in Appendix C.

In this book, however, I go back to the origins of single-source research, and the data I publish and analyze are based on household purchasing and concerned with the relationship between the identified advertising for specific brands and the sales of those brands. In other words, I am primarily concerned with pure single-source research, as defined in this chapter.

Repeat-Purchase Packaged Goods

This book is devoted to ongoing campaigns for established brands, although it does not exclude reintroductions and improvements, known as restages or repositionings, that take place with most brands every three or four years. Nor does it exclude launches of new brands. However, the emphasis on continuous campaigns whose budgets do not vary widely from year to year means that this book describes a different field from that examined by the study published in 1991 based on research by Information Resources Inc. (IRI), which reviewed 293 tests of increased advertising expenditure.[7] The IRI study is discussed in Appendix C.

I am concerned in this work exclusively with repeat-purchase packaged goods, described in Britain as fast-moving consumer goods or FMCG. These are mass-market, low-priced products for household consumption bought in supermarkets, food stores, drugstores, and mass merchandisers (e.g., Wal-Mart). They are sold to homemakers who are mostly, although not invariably, women. More than 15 percent of American households have a male homemaker rather than a female one. (As a broad average, Nielsen consumer panel data show that about 20 percent of household buying is done by men.) What is more, men are present, doing the shopping alone or accompanying the lady of the house, when a third or more of all household shopping takes place. In this book, I am nevertheless going to follow the widely established convention of referring to the average homemaker as "she" rather than "he," but readers should be aware that the man is often an important decision-maker, either as homemaker or as someone interested in household affairs.

Advertising plays a pivotal role in selling repeat-purchase packaged goods, making such products very important to the advertising business, although they account in total for less than 40 percent of all advertising expenditure in the United States. Manufacturers of these products are the most knowledgeable and sophisticated advertisers of all, with the result that we know more about advertising for repeat-purchase packaged goods than we do about that in any other field, with the exception of direct response (mainly mail-order advertising), which by its nature lends itself to precise quantification. Single-source research is employed virtually exclusively to measure the sales of brands in repeat-purchase categories.

The Measurement of Advertising Effects

In this book, advertising effects are measured by national figures specially tabulated from the Nielsen Household Panel. A full year's data have been used, although six months would have been enough in many cases. Advertisers will be conscious that a year or even six months of national advertising is a high price to pay for confirming the effectiveness or ineffectiveness of any advertising campaign. Any alternative, however, to measuring the short-term sales effect of advertising produces a much worse outcome: in fact, a dangerous one, because of the vast waste of media dollars that might result. In the past, ineffective campaigns have sometimes run for years, leading to a total waste of substantial sums of money. And even when sales were maintained, nothing could be known about the reasons for the success except misleading inferences about the supposed effectiveness of the campaigns.

Pure single-source research is unique and it represents a research breakthrough. This book is an analysis of what has been discovered; it is not an attempt to sell the Nielsen system. Indeed, it is by no means certain that the Nielsen service will continue in any form in the future; it was originally set up on a quasi-experimental basis.

Whether or not pure single-source research eventually becomes a part of the American market research scene depends on the ability of advertisers to appreciate its great value. However, it is difficult to accept that advertisers would prefer to risk wasting money on bad advertising than to spend money to discover definitively whether their advertising is bad or good.

In my opinion, a search for alternative systems that might yield equally sensitive and accurate information on the effects of advertising would be a generally futile endeavor. The only possible exception is the Attitudiual Short-Term Advertising Strength (ASTAS) system developed in Denmark, which is discussed in Chapter 3. The American research industry managed to drill a vast number of dry holes during the quarter-century that passed between the first use of pure single-source research in the 1960s and its eventual national implementation by Nielsen in the 1990s. Further exploration of alternatives is likely to result in nothing but more dry holes. Advertisers will thus have to pay the price for neglecting the contributions that pure single-source research can make toward improving virtually all their advertising and marketing activities.

By far the most practicable idea for exploiting pure single-source research would be to devise a system of calculating the sales effect of advertising from test-market data, but using test-market data would require special household panels in a number of restricted areas, using the exceptionally rigorous data-collection systems described in this book. This would involve heavy start-up costs, but the financial balance after a time would be favorable, because of a regional rather than national media investment. I feel very strongly that this is the direction that pure single-source research should take in the future. A permanent service providing national data should follow the success of such a test-market program; the latter should of course also continue for the basic evaluation of campaigns.

Beginning in 2004, a number of research organizations (including A.C. Nielsen) introduced tests of a large piece of pure single-source research code-named Project Apollo: an even more ambitious program than the work reported in this book. There is as yet no evidence that it is able to garner enough support from the advertising industry to make it a continuous service. The prospect is, regrettably, not too optimistic.

Notes

1. John Philip Jones and Jan S. Slater, *What's in a Name? Advertising and the Concept of Brands,* 2nd ed. (Armonk, NY: M.E. Sharpe, 2003), pp. 143–145.

2. John Philip Jones, *The Ultimate Secrets of Advertising* (Thousand Oaks, CA: Sage Publications, 2002).

3. John Philip Jones, *Does It Pay to Advertise? Cases Illustrating Successful Brand Advertising* (New York: Macmillan-Lexington Books, 1989), p. 12.

4. James Spaeth and Michael Hess, "Single-Source Data . . . the Missing Pieces," in *Fulfilling the Promise of Electronic Single-Source Data* (New York: Advertising Research Foundation Conference, June 1989), p. 142.

5. Colin McDonald, "What Is the Short-Term Effect of Advertising?" in *Effective Frequency: The Relationship Between Frequency and Advertising Effectiveness,* ed. Michael Naples, pp. 86–88 (New York: Association of National Advertisers, 1979).

6. These definitions were provided by J. Walker Smith, Lynn S. Whitton, Alice K. Sylvester, Stephen A. Douglas, and Scott N. Johnson in *New Insights into Single-Source Data* (New York: Advertising Research Foundation Conference, July 1988), pp. 16, 24, 68, 76, 114; Lawrence N. Gold, Allan L. Baldinger, Brian M. Shea, Blair Peters, Marilyn Henninger and Edward Dittus, Andrew M. Tarshis, James Spaeth and Michael Hess, and Beth Axelrad in *Fulfilling the Promise of Single-Source Data* (New York: Advertising Research Foundation Conference, June 1989), pp. 6, 28, 54, 75, 86, 120, 143, 171; and Joseph R. Russo, *Behavioral Research and Single-Source Data* (New York: paper presented at Advertising Research Foundation Conference, June 1990), p. 11.

7. Michael J. Naples, Randall S. Smith, Leonard M. Lodish, Beth Lubetkin, Josh McQueen, Larry Bisno, Horst Stipp, and Andrew M. Tarshis, *Breakthrough Marketplace Advertising Research for Bottom Line Results* (New York: paper presented at Advertising Research Foundation Conference, November 1991).

2

The Short-Term Effect of Advertising
Passing Through the Gate

This book provides strong evidence that advertising is capable of producing a pronounced effect on consumer purchases of a brand within a short period (generally measured as seven days) after its exposure. This short-term effect varies a great deal according to the advertising used. It can be measured post hoc. Since one advertisement does most of the work, the effect must come substantially from the advertisement itself: from the creative idea within it.

Proponents of direct-response (mail order) advertising would not be in any way surprised by the above paragraph. Direct-response advertising works in no other fashion, and it is the immediate measurable response from such advertising that made possible what Claude Hopkins, an important early practitioner of mail order, called scientific advertising.

There is, however, much less agreement that the same principles and methods of operation apply to advertising for other types of goods and services and in particular that for repeat-purchase packaged goods. The problem was and is measurability. These types of products are not sold by the manufacturer off the page and delivered to the consumer by mail. They are distributed through third parties: in some cases both wholesalers and retailers, and in other cases retailers alone. With this indirect

13

relationship between the advertiser and the end consumer, it has always been difficult to establish a clear link between the exposure of an advertisement and the purchase of a brand across the checkout at the store—and no link, no measurability.

Difficulty of measurement is an important background reason for the way in which the brand image doctrine has been so strongly supported over the years by many thoughtful advertising people. Their thinking is that, since they find it virtually impossible to see any change in sales immediately after advertising appears, then something else must be taking place. In fact, it is optimistically assumed that the advertising is working indirectly—and perhaps also powerfully—to strengthen the image attributes and associations of the brand and that the benefit will be seen in the long term. This idea remains strong today with sometimes dangerous consequences. It plays an important role in reassuring many advertisers who are running ineffective campaigns that everything is all right after all.

Some analysts still believe that all advertising effects are no more than the accumulated delayed effects of advertisements that have been exposed weeks, months, and years before. I believe that this doctrine is wrong or, at the very least, gravely incomplete.

Colin McDonald, whose pioneering work was described in Chapter 1, surprised the professional world by the strength of the immediate advertising effects that he demonstrated. It is therefore astonishing that a quarter-century passed before pure single-source research was extended on a major scale and with the use of advanced technology. But eventually a large piece of such research was carried out in the United States in 1991 and 1992 by the A.C. Nielsen Company. My contribution to the enterprise was partly in the planning of the research method and more especially in interpreting the findings. These were released in the first edition of this book, published in 1995, and also in many journal articles.[1] Like McDonald, I found powerful effects immediately after the advertising.

Short-Term Advertising Strength

The Nielsen system of single-source research was based on Nielsen's ongoing Household Panel, a properly drawn sample of 40,000 households across the United States, in which every purchase of regularly bought brands is logged with hand-held scanners. In each home, the shopper uses the scanner to read the Universal Product Code (UPC) on each package bought, thus recording details of brand name, variety, and pack size. The shopper also punches in manually the date, the price, simple details of any promotional offers, the name of the store, and the identity of the individual doing the shopping. The information that has been fed into the scanner is sent to Nielsen by a simple automatic process over the public telephone lines. The data gathering is continuous: longitudinal, to use the technical language of statistics. The scanner system is data collection of a highly sophisticated type. Nevertheless, it represented only one of three pieces of information needed for pure single-source research.

The second process of data collection covered television viewing. This initial Nielsen study concentrated on television alone, although later studies by other research organizations also covered magazines. (These are discussed in Chapter 3.) Nielsen selected a representative subset of 2,000 homes from the Household Panel and attached a meter to every television set in each home to record when it was switched on and to which channel. The viewing of individual family members was not recorded, but "People Meters" enabled this to be done for the A.C. Nielsen single-source research in Germany (also discussed in Chapter 3).

The third piece of research tackled the immense diversity of television viewing patterns: the large number of different channels viewed in each of 150 cities and regions in the United States. Nielsen used a system called Monitor Plus, which employs a series of television receiving stations that log all the advertising that appears, at fifteen-second intervals, in the twenty-three largest designated market areas (DMAs) in the United States, covering more than half the total population. Information is collected from all the main stations in these areas, both network and cable.

There were thus three different streams of information—on household purchasing, television viewing, and the identities of the advertised brands. I decided on a "window" of seven days as the period during which a short-term advertising effect is assumed to be felt. Since the date when the brand was purchased was collected in the scanner, it was relatively easy to identify whether advertising for that same brand had entered—or had *not* entered—the household during the preceding seven days. Nielsen took immense pains to devise the computer programs to generate the information that I specified. (This book is dedicated to the three experts who achieved this feat.)

Figure 2.1   **Ad Households and Adless Households**

Purchases in ad households *minus* purchases in adless
households = purchases driven by advertising.

The basic idea behind the research was the concept of "ad households" and "adless households," illustrated in Figure 2.1.

A subtle but important characteristic of these two collections of households is that the groups were different *for every single purchase occasion.* With each purchase of any brand, the 2,000 households in the panel
formed themselves into unique combinations of ad households and adless
households, plus a third group who had not purchased the brand at all at
this time. For the next purchase of a brand, the groups were mixed totally differently.

The tabulation of the data was extremely complicated, but this was a
vital part of the process. We were examining constantly changing combinations of the same collection of 2,000 households. The advantage of
this system was that it guaranteed the homogeneity of the subsamples.
The presence or absence of advertising was the sole variable distinguishing the subsamples on every occasion that the brand was bought. Here
are examples of what this meant in practice.

Buying took place at different times of the year, during various seasonal highs and lows depending on the product category. In the high
season, both the ad households and adless households were buying a
great deal, and the only difference between them was the presence or
absence of advertising beforehand. It worked in a similar way in the low
season, when people were buying less. Buying also took place accom-
panied by sales promotions and unaccompanied by sales promotions.
When promotions were in operation, they attracted both ad households
and adless households, and again the only difference between them was
the presence or absence of advertising before the purchase. The same
was true of purchases unaccompanied by sales promotions.

The constantly changing grouping of ad households and adless households was a totally different system from one based on a matched pair of

permanent, geographically separated subpanels: the method used by the American research company Information Resources Inc. (IRI) for its BehaviorScan panels. The research in France, discussed in Chapter 3, employed this latter method.[2]

The measure of advertising effect I developed was based on a brand's market share *measured in purchase occasions* and not purchase volume. The former is a sharper way of signaling advertising effects. The name I gave the system is short-term advertising strength (STAS), and it has three elements:

- *baseline STAS*: The brand's market share in the households that had received no television advertising for it during the seven days before the purchase took place.
- s*timulated STAS*: The brand's market share in the households that had received at least one television advertisement for it during these previous seven days.
- *STAS differential*: The difference between the baseline STAS and the stimulated STAS. This is normally indexed on the baseline, which has a value of 100. The STAS differential index is the measure of the short-term sales gain (or loss) generated by a brand's advertising. It is a mathematical expression of the difference between the purchasing of the two groups in Figure 2.1, the ad households and the adless households.

The STAS measures are described in Figure 2.2.

A brand's STAS differential is an average for all the separate purchases of a brand across a year; my research was mostly based on the twelve months of 1991. The research measured a total of seventy-eight advertised brands (with purchasing data for an additional sixty-two unadvertised ones). I covered twelve product categories, with a total of more than 110,000 purchase occasions: an average of about 1,400 per brand. These are detailed in Table 2.1. My categories were chosen to be typical of the field of repeat-purchase packaged goods as a whole and to offer a reasonable spread of products. These product groups vary in their advertising intensity and in the number of advertised brands in each. A very important point about these categories is that television is by far their most important advertising medium. This is the case for the majority of repeat-purchase packaged goods, but there are exceptions (notably cigarettes and hard liquor). Each product field was given a letter

Figure 2.2   **STAS Measures for Brand Code Named AL**

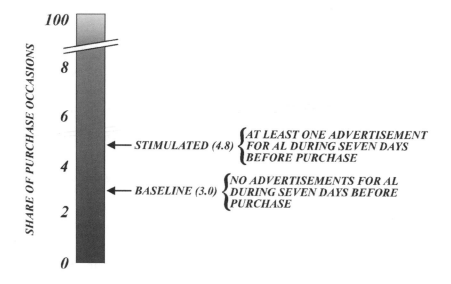

code, as shown in Table 2.1. The third column shows the upper limit of the statistical sample: the number of purchases among the 2,000 households recorded in 1991 in each product category. In packaged detergents (category A) for instance, the 8,385 purchases show that the average household bought the product more than four times (8,385 divided by 2,000). (Table 2.1 does *not* show the subsamples for each brand, which indicate its relative importance. The largest brand in category A has its data derived from 3,668 purchases; and the smallest brand, from 680 purchases. The details of the subsamples for each brand do not add anything to this research and they have not been included in this book.)

In each product category I concentrated on the leading brands. There are about a dozen of these in most product fields, the smallest of which have shares of 2 percent and sometimes less. In each field, I have coded every brand with a second letter; for instance, in packaged detergents, the brands are AA, AB, AC, and so forth. In some cases, two brands in a category share a common brand name, although the product formula is different. In these cases, a second brand with the same name as one already recorded is coded by repeating the first brand's identifying letter, such as AA and AAA, BH and BHH. In one case, there is a third identified variant; I have named this LCCC, to distinguish it from LC and LCC.

Table 2.1

Categories and Sample Sizes

Code	Category	Number of purchases
A	Packaged detergents	8,385
B	Liquid detergents	6,713
C	Bar soaps	10,562
D	Shampoos	9.361
E	Toilet tissue	11,427
F	Ice cream	9,726
G	Mayonnaise	8,094
H	Peanut butter	9,368
J	Ground coffee	8,083
K	Diet carbonated soft drinks	9,069
L	Breakfast cereals	11,320
M	Analgesics	9,032

Source: A.C. Nielsen.

In each category, there is also a group called All Others: a bloc of small brands not separately analyzed, and aggregated into a share of market covering sales not accounted for by the named brands. These aggregations are usually under 20 percent, but they are larger for categories D, F, L, and M, which are very fragmented.

This research covers eighty advertised brands, of which full data are available for seventy-eight. Most analyses are therefore based on this total.

The simplest way to show the sharp and wide-ranging effects of advertising is by dividing the seventy-eight brands into a number of more or less equal groups and calculating the average STAS differential for each.[3] I ranked all the brands by the size of their individual STAS, then divided them into ten separate blocks (of 7-8-8-8-8-8-8-8-8-7 brands), known technically as deciles. I then averaged the STAS for each decile, with the results shown in Table 2.2. Table 2.2 also indicates the sales index over the medium term (i.e., over the course of a year).

Table 2.2 shows that at the top end of my sample of brands, the immediate effect of advertising is very powerful, the strongest 10 percent of advertisements boosting sales by an average of 136 percent. Seventy percent of advertisements cause some immediate sales increase. But 30 percent of advertisements are associated with a *reduction* in sales. I do not believe that these advertisements at the bottom end actually cause

Table 2.2

Decile Analysis of STAS (Nielsen seventy-eight brands)

Rank	Average STAS differential	Medium-term sales index
Top	236	182
Ninth	164	121
Eighth	139	113
Seventh	121	109
Sixth	116	104
Fifth	108	98
Fourth	103	95
Third	97	90
Second	89	84
Bottom	73	69
Average	124	106

sales to go down because they are so positively awful. The better explanation is that the advertising is not strong enough to protect the brands from the more powerful campaigns of the competition when the brand and the competition are advertised at the same time.

Table 2.2 also shows what happened to my seventy-eight brands over the course of a year. This medium-term effect is weaker than the STAS effect, although in total the sales of the brands advanced by 6 percent, a gain made at the expense of store brands and generics.

One extremely important point is that a brand must generate a short-term effect before it can produce any further effect. Therefore a positive STAS differential *acts as a gatekeeper* to medium- and long-term growth.

Brands with a positive STAS differential can suffer from temporary downs when they are unadvertised. But if there are few gaps in a brand's advertising schedule (i.e., if there is a high degree of media continuity), brands with a strong STAS can improve their market shares over the course of a year. In this book, I measure this medium-term change in sales on the basis of change in market share (to eliminate the effect of seasonality). Market share in the first quarter of 1991 is the base level (indexed as 100), and the change in share over the course of the year is measured by the average of the second, third, and fourth quarters.

The medium-term effect of advertising is brought about by a repetition of the sales ups that are generated by the STAS differential, minus the downs when the brand is unadvertised. A positive STAS differential can lead to a market share improvement if there is sufficient media expenditure to buy a reasonably continuous schedule, which in effect protects the brand against the positive STAS of competitive brands. The importance of this point is that in many categories, a single share point can yield, at manufacturers' prices, $100 million of revenue and sometimes more.

Along with the effect of media continuity, the internal momentum of the brand adds a further long-term drive. This momentum is partly, although not exclusively, derived from previous advertising, and its force differs by brand. As a broad generalization, large brands have a stronger internal momentum than small brands do, for the simple reason that they have a higher frequency of purchase than small brands. (See Chapter 11.) The internal momentum represents a scale economy of large brands, and it is one of the reasons I have isolated the large brands into a separate group in this study. They are named Beta brands.

I have divided my seventy-eight brands into four groups as follows:

1. *Alpha One*—advertising that works. Brands with a positive STAS differential that show a market share improvement. There are twenty-six of these, representing a projected 33 percent of the total. (See Chapter 7.)
2. *Alpha Two*—advertising that stops working. These are brands with a positive STAS differential which show no medium-term market share improvement. There are nineteen of these, representing a projected 24 percent of the total. (See Chapter 8.)
3. *Beta*—advertising that works in some cases. These are large brands (those with a 10 percent market share or more), for which advertising plays a basically defensive role. Advertising works in seven and possibly as many as ten cases (projected 13 percent), but does not work in a further ten cases (projected 13 percent). (See Chapter 9.)
4. *Gamma*—advertising that does not work. Any sales increases are caused by factors other than advertising. There are thirteen brands in this group, representing a projected 17 percent of the total. (See Chapter 10.)

The projected 70 percent of advertising that has a short-term effect is derived from Alpha One, Alpha Two, and the successful Beta brands. The projected 46 percent of advertising that has both a short- and medium-term effect is derived from only the Alpha One and successful Beta brands.

There is good evidence from the Alpha One, Alpha Two, and Beta brands about how the advertising stimuli influence sales. At the upper levels of the STAS differential, there is an association between higher STAS differential and higher medium-term sales, presumably because of the repeat purchase that is generated by the more powerful short-term stimulus. And as a general rule covering all brands with a positive STAS differential, greater amounts of advertising expenditure will also produce greater medium-term sales. Over the period of a year, advertising provides a double drive—qualitative (i.e., from STAS) and quantitative (i.e., from media continuity). In other words, advertisers can expect results when they spend money to expose effective, creative advertising. Readers will remember the example of brand code-named AL (Figure 2.2.). This showed a short-term sales improvement of 60 percent. Over the course of a year this brand increased by 14 percent, a very substantial increase in a large country like the United States.

Advertised Versus Unadvertised Brands

The most decisive way of evaluating the overall effect of advertising is to examine the relative performance of advertised versus unadvertised brands. This research provides a large amount of information on the progress of both groups over the course of a year, and I shall examine these groups according to their consumer prices and sales growth (using data provided by Nielsen).

In my calculations, the price of a brand is the average of the amount paid by consumers for each purchase. This price is a product of the manufacturer's list price minus any temporary promotional offers. The most convenient and meaningful way of comparing the prices of brands, both within their category and across categories, is to compare each brand's price with the average of brands in its own category. If its average price is one-fourth higher than the overall category average, I have indexed the brand as 125.

Sales growth or decline is measured over the course of 1991 and is derived from quarterly data on market shares, to avoid seasonal influences. And (as explained earlier) I have based each brand's growth or decline on its market share in the first quarter of 1991, expressed as 100. The sales increase (or decrease) over the rest of the year is measured by indexing the brand's average share over the second, third, and fourth quarters.[4] This is not a perfect way of calculating the change in sales of

Table 2.3

Advertised and Unadvertised Brands: Growth and Decline

	Advertised brands		Unadvertised brands	
	Number	Average sales index	Number	Average sales index
Growing brands	42	123	33	119
Declining brands	38	87	29	88

a brand, but it is reasonably reliable as well as being easy to calculate and understand.

The 142 brands analyzed in this book are split between advertised and unadvertised brands: eighty (56 percent) are advertised and sixty-two (44 percent) are not. (Nielsen measured whether or not the brands were advertised.) The market shares of most brands do not change very widely over time, despite their short-term volatility. However, many increase marginally over a year, and to balance this increase many others go down by a small amount. This overall balance holds for both market shares and raw sales. Product categories are generally stable in absolute terms so that the sales gains of some brands tend to be balanced by the losses of others.

In this study, I found that seventy-five brands (53 percent) gained share over the course of the year, while sixty-seven brands (47 percent) suffered a corresponding loss. One surprising finding, illustrated in Table 2.3, is that there is almost the same proportion of growing brands in the unadvertised group as among the advertised brands (in both cases, slightly more advances than declines). This is the type of finding that might lead to earthquakes on Madison Avenue. However and fortunately for advertising practitioners, it also demonstrates that superficial "top line" or summarized measures of the effectiveness of advertising can be more misleading than enlightening.

To understand this comparison properly, we must look at four additional factors. First—as might be expected—the advertised brands are much larger. The average market share of all advertised brands is higher than that of all unadvertised brands. The average share of the rising advertised brands is 7.1 percent; that of the rising unadvertised brands is 4.8, a level one-third lower. As a general rule, brands with the larger market shares tend to be less volatile and also more profitable (in absolute and relative terms) than brands with the smaller shares. The better margins of larger brands are the result of scale economies of various types.

The second point is that the penetration of the advertised brands is much higher than that of the unadvertised ones. Over the course of 1991, the average proportion of households buying one of the advertised brands analyzed in this book was 17.2 percent; the average for the unadvertised brands was 10.1 percent (41 percent lower). For most brands, advertising drives penetration.

The third point is that the advertised brands command higher prices than the unadvertised ones. The average rising advertised brand has a price index of 106: that is, it is 6 percent above the category average. The average figure for the rising unadvertised brands is 93, or 7 percent below the category average. Another way of making the same comparison is to say that the advertised brands were priced on average 14 percent above the unadvertised (13 percentaged on 93).

One of the reasons unadvertised brands are generally priced low is that most of them have to be driven by promotions to compensate for their lack of advertising. Promotions are very expensive and tend to bite severely into a brand's profitability. It is also likely that many unadvertised brands are of slightly inferior quality to the advertised ones, and their manufacturing costs could therefore be slightly lower. Unadvertised brands also save money by the very fact of being unadvertised. But even taking into account the savings on both raw materials and advertising, I believe that the unadvertised brands, with their lower prices, are generally less profitable to manufacturers than advertised brands, with their higher prices. Promotions take too much out of a brand's margins, which is another way of saying that larger brands benefit from scale economies.[5]

The fourth point about the advertised and unadvertised brands is that it is inadequate merely to count the numbers of growing and declining brands. We must examine the amounts by which they grew and declined. There is a modest but significant difference between the advertised and unadvertised brands, as shown in Table 2.3. We can express the slightly better sales performance of the advertised brands by saying that on average, their sales growth was 3 percent above that of the unadvertised ones (123 percentaged on 119).

In summary, comparing the advertised and unadvertised brands reveals the same proportion of growing unadvertised brands as growing advertised ones. But the growing advertised brands were 14 percent higher in price and likely to be more profitable. The growing advertised brands increased in volume by 3 percent more than the unadvertised brands. Thus, in value terms, the growing advertised brands were 17 percent ahead of the growing unadvertised ones (114 multiplied by 103 percent). Finally, and not least importantly, the advertised brands were larger and had a much higher household penetration. They were probably also more stable than the unadvertised ones.

There is nothing surprising about these conclusions. But there is one thing they do not say. Advertising effects may be both durable and qualitative (e.g., affecting quality perceptions of a brand), but they are also highly selective. Advertising works very well with some brands, but not at all with others.

One important group of unadvertised brands is store brands. Nine of these are reviewed in Chapter 9. These brands as a group slightly improved their overall share over the course of the year. The special strength of store brands in the retail trade gives them a quality similar to an internal momentum: that is, they have the backing of the store whose name is associated with them. However, the consumer price of store brands was on average 29 percent below the Beta brands. To the storekeeper, although store brands may yield a higher percentage profit than manufacturers' brands, this percentage is applied to a much lower base cost. As a result, the retailer's profit for each unit of store brands will in most cases be lower than that from manufacturers' brands. It should also be remembered that the sales value of store brands is much less than for manufacturers' labels.

Notes

1. John Philip Jones, "Advertising's Woes and Advertising Accountability," *Admap*, September 1994, pp. 24–77; "Advertising Exposure Effects Under a Microscope," *Admap*, February 1995, pp. 28–31; "Single-Source Research Begins to Fulfil Its Promise," *Journal of Advertising Research*, May/June 1995, pp. 9–16; "Single-Source Is the Key to Proving Advertising's Short-Term Effects," *Admap*, June 1995, pp. 33–34; "Is Advertising Still Salesmanship?" *Journal of Advertising Research,* May/June 1997, pp. 9–15.

2. IRI was critical of my method because I did *not* use permanent and separate matched samples. From our published exchanges, I am not totally sure that IRI understands how my system works. See articles in *Journal of Advertising Research* by Gary Schroeder, Bruce C. Richardson, and Avu Sankaralingam, "Validating STAS Using BehaviorScan," July/August 1997, pp. 33–43; Leonard M. Lodish, "Point of View: J.P. Jones and M.H. Blair on Measuring Advertising Effects—Another Point of View," September/October 1997, pp. 75–79; John Philip Jones, "Point of View: STAS and BehaviorScan—Yet Another View," March/April 1998, pp. 51–53; and Leonard M. Lodish, "STAS and BehaviorScan—It's Just Not That Simple," March/April 1998, pp. 54–56.

3. As explained, I based this analysis on seventy-eight usable brands. I had to reject two brands because their STAS numbers were outliers: figures so high that they were off the map. To include these would have distorted the averages. The two brands are small, and I assume that the freak observations were the result of statistical error.

4. There is a small number of brands whose index of growth remained at 100—in other words, no change—and I included these in the growing rather than the declining group. My reasoning was that, in a competitive environment, to hold one's position is a reasonable measure of success. This is especially true of the brands with the higher shares of market, which are in an essentially defensive position and which I have named in this book the Beta brands.

5. This point is elaborated in John Philip Jones, "The Double Jeopardy of Sales Promotions," *Harvard Business Review*, September–October 1990, pp. 145–152.

—————— 3 ——————

The Rapid Spread of Pure
Single-Source Research

Even before the first edition of *When Ads Work* was published, I revealed some of my findings, which stirred up much interest and some controversy in the United States and abroad. One of the first countries to express positive interest in the research was Japan, and a leading Japanese market researcher visited in me in Syracuse, New York, in early 1995. (I remember the time of year because of the snow on the ground, which caught him unprepared!) I heard nothing more from Japan, but some years later an English researcher told me something about the extensive single-source research carried out there by Densu, the largest advertising agency in Tokyo: research the agency had been using on a proprietary basis and has never published.

The use of my technique in other countries was more fully acknowledged, and this chapter is devoted to some of the details of this foreign work.

Germany and Britain

Some months after the findings of the American research were published, I was commissioned by the German advertising agencies' association, Gesamtverband Werbeagenturen, to carry out a similar piece of work in cooperation with the A.C. Nielsen company in Germany. We

Table 3.1

Three-Country Decile Analysis of STAS Differentials

Rank	United States, 1991 78 brands Nielsen	Germany, 1993 28 brands Nielsen	Britain, 1986–90 67 brands Adlab
Top	236	154	184
Ninth	164	127	129
Eighth	139	116	119
Seventh	121	108	114
Sixth	116	106	110
Fifth	108	101	107
Fourth	103	100	102
Third	97	98	98
Second	89	92	93
Bottom	73	83	73

used data from 1993 and 1994, and although the statistical foundation was substantial, the overall scale of the research was about half that of the American study. However, the use of "People Meters," identifying viewing by homemakers and other family members, represented an advance on the technique used in the American investigation.[1]

After another short interval, Colin McDonald, the pioneer of pure single-source research, gained access to the British Adlab database, which covered four and a half years' experience of five important product categories. Overall the size of the Adlab investigation was larger than my American study by a factor of more than 2 to 1.[2] McDonald tabulated and interpreted his Adlab data in the same way as I had carried out the original American study. It is instructive to compare the distribution of short-term advertising strength (STAS) effects in Germany and Britain with the original work in the United States. We see this comparison in Table 3.1.

The distribution of the figures has approximately the same shape in the three countries: certainly the similarities are greater than the differences. The range of advertising effects from Germany is more compact than that in the United States, with less extreme numbers at top and bottom. The British figures fall somewhere between the American and the German. However, in all three countries the immediate effect of advertising on sales is shown to be very large, certainly in the top deciles, and in all three there is a wide range of variation. Significantly, in all three countries, 30 percent of campaigns are ineffective.

Table 3.2

First Two-Country Quintile Analysis of STAS Differentials

Rank	United States, 1991 78 brands Nielsen	France, 1996 144 brands BehaviorScan
Top	198	200
Fourth	130	139
Third	112	117
Second	100	99
Bottom	82	77

More Countries, More Replication

The Information Resources Inc. BehaviorScan system differs from my own research in that BehaviorScan uses permanent and geographically separated household panels, while I use a single national panel in which the ad households, adless households, and nonbuying households change with every purchase occasion and thus represent different groupings of the same basic panel of 2,000 homes.

IRI has never taken kindly to my system, claiming its own to have greater scientific purity.[3] I was nevertheless very surprised to see that when it published a range of STAS differentials, its findings were close to mine. The published BehaviorScan research (Table 3.2) comes from France.[4] The data in Table 3.2 were analyzed into quintiles (in which the STAS figures are ranked from highest to lowest and then broken down into five blocks). I have recomputed the American data from Table 3.1 in the same way.

In the Scandinavian countries, market analysts have been both energetic and imaginative in making STAS calculations using relatively simple and inexpensive data-collection systems. Since the Scandinavian markets are small in absolute terms—although not in marketing sophistication—research companies there are unable to afford the high cost of the technical equipment used for collecting data electronically, as can be done in countries as large as the United States, Germany, and Britain.

In Denmark, Flemming Hansen of the Copenhagen Business School, working with the Taylor Nelson Sofres Gallup research organization, developed a system using 6,700 personal interviews to measure both

Table 3.3

Second Two-Country Quintile Analysis of STAS Differentials

Rank	United States, 1991 78 brands Nielsen	Denmark, 1999 23 brands Gallup
Top	198	246
Fourth	130	196
Third	112	154
Second	100	122
Bottom	82	91

brand purchasing and advertising exposure, signaled by awareness of advertising for a brand. Hansen found an ingenious way of eliminating "phantom awareness" (i.e., imaginary awareness of advertising that had not actually appeared).[5] He called his measure attitudinal STAS, or ASTAS. His range of quintiles is shown in Table 3.3. This describes twenty-three Danish brands, and it is another example of broad similarity with the findings of the original American research. The slightly higher Danish readings are a result of the different method of data collection. Hansen provided a separate ASTAS figure for each brand from television and magazine advertising separately. The magazine figures were based on small samples, which may account for the fact they are nearly all higher than those from television. Nevertheless, magazines are a powerful advertising medium in Denmark, where people are relatively highly educated and read a great deal.

In Norway, Thorolf Helgesen of the Norwegian School of Management, with Morten Micalsen of the Norwegian Gallup Research Institute, decided to revisit Colin McDonald's 1966 method of collecting data with the use of paper-and-pencil diaries filled in by homemakers. Using this technique, researchers carried out a study of 860 Norwegian households over a two-month period at the end of 1997.[6] The analysts examined thirty-three brands, and they found the STAS differentials to range between the two extremes of 329 and 55. Five of the thirty-three scores were negative. Again, there is a similarity with the range of the American data, although the findings from Norway show stronger advertising effects, almost certainly a result of the different method of data collection.

Like Hansen in Denmark, Helgesen and Micalsen also measured the STAS from magazine advertising and found results that were even more positive than the Danish ones. Like Denmark, Norway has a powerful magazine press; and also as in Denmark, there is a high level of education, and people read.

At the time when the Norwegians were getting their research under way, I fortuitously gained access to a large historical American database, from which I was able to calculate STAS figures from magazine advertising. This information came from the Starch organization, a company that has been exploring the readership of print advertising since the 1920s. The data I received were derived from studies of 45,000 advertisements in the *Saturday Evening Post* and *Life* over the years 1944 through 1960.

For each of the magazines in the study and immediately after each issue appeared, Starch measured the household purchasing of specific brands. This was done both in households that had received the issues of these journals in which the brands were advertised and also in households that had not been exposed to the advertisements. This method made it possible to connect the reception of the advertisements to the purchase of the same brands: in effect, pure single-source research.

Using the arithmetic of my STAS system, with the baseline indexed at 100, the average STAS differential for all the measured magazine advertisements was 119 (a finding significant at the 99 percent probability level). This figure was calculated from all the brands in the sample for which suitable information was available—seventy-three brands that had appeared in 707 different advertisements.[7]

In my original American research into television viewing and brand buying, the STAS figure for all the brands together averaged 124 (Table 2.2 in Chapter 2). This average measured all amounts of advertising received before the brand was bought. As I shall discuss in Chapter 5, most of the effect of advertising comes from households that have received only a single advertisement. For these single-advertisement households, the STAS differential averaged 118. The Starch magazine data are based on single-advertisement measures. This means that the average responsiveness of consumer purchasing to a single advertisement on television (measured by Nielsen) is *virtually the same* as the average responsiveness to a single magazine advertisement (measured by Starch).

The seven studies I have just discussed were all based on pure single-source research. Interesting supplementary work was carried out by Michael von Gonten and James Donius, who used the same Nielsen Household Panel data as I did, but they analyzed the information in a totally different way. They did, however, produce conclusions similar to my own.

Von Gonten and Donius used as their main measure a brand's penetration: the percentage of households buying it during a defined period.[8] Their research tracks penetration growth from a selected starting point (e.g., January 1) measured at zero. This nil-penetration refers only to the beginning of the research period. The new buyers in the period will only rarely be true first-time buyers; they will be mostly repeat buyers from earlier periods, but this distinction is ignored because the research concept is based on penetration growth, and to measure this it is best to start at zero. From this starting point, penetration for an established brand increases in a relatively smooth upward path, or trajectory. This trajectory serves as the baseline used by von Gonten and Donius when they measure the boosts or "upticks" that result from various marketing activities, notably media advertising and sales promotions.

The effect of these stimuli is measured as an upward step in the trajectory above the established trend. In any week this trend is measured as 1 (a number chosen simply for purposes of comparison). The analysts' conclusions from the research are as follows, and each point is important to the present discussion:

- Effective commercials average around 1.85 times as much (increase in) penetration as would be achieved if off-air during that specific week. The high end of the observed range is around 4 to 5 times.
- Specific executions have the capacity to differ in effect, even when they are simple "pool-outs."
- The effect is observed in the week in which advertising airs and is absent in off-air weeks.[9]

Von Gonten and Donius also reveal interesting data on repeat purchase and subsequent additional purchase, providing insights into the longer-term effects of advertising.

All the evidence described so far comes from the various categories of repeat-purchase packaged goods. In the past, what has been learned about advertising in these tough, advertising-intensive, and highly competitive product fields has been applied in a general fashion to many other advertised categories. There is no reason to doubt that the lessons from the research described here can also be applied widely. But this assumption should not be taken as an excuse for not carrying out parallel investigations in such important fields as travel, financial services, telecommunications, and the many and varied types of goods with a high ticket price, notably automobiles. Some work has been done, but it is unpublished.

How Many Brands Pass Through the Gate?

I have given evidence supporting the proposition that advertising is capable of producing a pronounced effect on consumer purchases of a brand within a short period (generally measured as seven days) after its exposure. This short-term effect varies a great deal according to the advertising used. It can be measured post hoc.

This evidence comes from six different countries and seven separate investigations. Six of these are based on pure single-source research, conducted longitudinally. These studies examined a total of 446 separate brands and related household buying to advertising received immediately beforehand. Each brand study was derived from (plus or minus) 1,000 statistical observations. The statistical foundation for my conclusions is a total not far short of half a million separate pieces of data.

I believe that the strength and consistency of this battery of mutually supporting studies have now pulled the rug from under the once-prevalent view that advertising cannot yield substantial immediate effects and that its only influence comes from the accumulation of multitudes of tiny effects that eventually produce something significant, or, in the words of a well-known monograph republished in 1998: "Advertising works over a period of time as a part of the gradual evolution of the individual's perceptions of a brand and its relations to other brands. The effect of a single isolated advertising exposure is likely to be minimal in most markets."[10] I am convinced that this hypothesis is based on very little truth and what truth it contains is misleading.

STAS indicates that a specific advertising campaign can produce an immediate and finite sales increase. But how do we prolong this effect? This is the next question raised by all the research summarized here: What is the level of immediate effect that should qualify an advertising campaign to pass through the gate—to be exposed further—with the aim of achieving a medium-term effect, possibly building up to a long-term effect? I believe that the initial cutoff level should be a STAS differential index of 120 and that campaigns that achieve STAS levels of

Table 3.4

Quintile Analysis of STAS Differentials and Average Size of Brand, United States: Seventy-eight Brands

Rank	STAS differential	Average share of market (percent)
Top	198	3.6
Fourth	130	6.9
Third	112	10.2
Second	110	12.1
Bottom	82	7.9

120 and more should be passed through the gate. There are, however, a few worthwhile campaigns that achieve a positive STAS differential in the marginal 105 to 119 range. Which of these should we also choose?

Table 3.4 helps us make this decision. It contains a quintile analysis of the STAS differentials of my original seventy-eight American brands. These are compared with the share of market of the average brand in each quintile.

The lower levels of positive STAS differentials are clearly associated with larger brands. This is a manifestation of a general characteristic of such brands: that they generally tend to perform rather sluggishly in the market place. But they nevertheless make an above-average contribution to a manufacturer's general overhead, and they also often yield above-average profit because they command an above-average consumer price (more precisely, an above-average *effective* consumer price, because they are promoted at a below-average rate). Bearing in mind these special characteristics of large brands, I believe that the brands with a STAS differential in the 105 to 119 range should be scrutinized, and those that command a significantly above-average consumer price should be allowed through the gate.

In my original study of seventy-eight American brands, thirty-one have a STAS differential index of 120 and above. These should all go through. Of the nineteen brands with differentials in the 105 to 119 range, seven sell at a consumer price more than 20 percent above their category average. I judge these also to be successful. Therefore, thirty-one brands plus seven brands, a total of thirty-eight—or about half my total of seventy-eight—should pass through the gate. The other pieces of pure single-source research described in this chapter tend to follow a broadly similar pattern. And we should remind ourselves of the words attributed variously to the important early advertisers William Hesketh Lever and John Wanamaker that half his advertising was wasted but he did not know which half. It seems that this generalization still holds, except that we *can* now identify which half works and which does not.

In Chapter 4 we shall return to the thirty-eight campaigns that pass through the gate and the forty that do not.

Notes

1. John Philip Jones, *When Ads Work: The German Version* (Frankfurt-am-Main: Gesamtverband Werbeagenturen GWAeV, 1995).

2. Colin McDonald, "How Frequently Should You Advertise?" *Admap*, July/August 1996, pp. 22–25.

3. See Chapter 2, n. 2.

4. Pascale Merzereau, Laurent Battais, and Laurent Spitzer, *Flighting Versus Pulsing Strategies on TV: Some BehaviorScan Findings* (Madrid: *asi* European Advertising Effectiveness Symposium, 1999).

5. Flemming Hansen and Charlotte Madsen, *Awareness and Attitudinal Sales Effects of TV Campaigns* (Copenhagen: Copenhagen Business School, 2000).

6. Thorolf Helgesen and Morten Micalsen, "Short-Term Advertising Strength: New Empirical Evidence from Norway," in *International Advertising: Realities and Myths*, ed. John Philip Jones, pp. 299–309 (Thousand Oaks, CA: Sage Publications, 2000).

7. John Philip Jones, "Consumer Purchasing, Starch and STAS: Does Magazine Advertising Produce an Immediate Effect?" in *How Advertising Works: The Role of Research*, ed. John Philip Jones, pp. 203–214 (Thousand Oaks, CA: Sage Publications, 1998).

8. Michael F. von Gonten and James F. Donius, "Advertising Exposure and Advertising Effects: New Panel-Based Findings," *Journal of Advertising Research*, July/August 1997, pp. 51–60.

9. Ibid., p. 59.

10. Alan Hedges, *Testing to Destruction* (London: Institute of Practitioners in Advertising, 1998), p. 26.

4

How a Short-Term Effect
Can Turn Into a
Medium-Term Effect

In an economically developed society like the United States, the most important and permanent feature of every type of commercial business is, not surprisingly, direct and indirect engagement with competitors. This makes itself felt both in preemptive activity and in responses to competitors' actions. And although there is nothing new about all this, competition provides the technical explanation for why the immediate effect of an advertising campaign sometimes can—but sometimes cannot—be extended into the medium term.

The STAS differential itself, being a measure of market share, is totally based on competition. If any campaign achieves a high STAS score, then it can be assumed that its behavioral effect is greater than that of campaigns for competitive brands that appeared more or less at the same time. Competition is an even more important factor over the medium term, because virtually every brand will have gaps in its media schedule, during which it will be vulnerable to competitors' advertising because it has been left unprotected. Avoiding gaps in the media schedule is directly relevant to the deployment of an advertising budget over time: a matter discussed in Chapter 5.

These concepts are summarized as follows: The short-term effect of an advertisement determines whether or not that advertisement will have a medium-term effect. A repetition of short-term effects over a period (normally twelve months)—effects felt exclusively during the periods when the brand is advertised—adds up to a medium-term effect. The medium-term effect is a net effect—sales gains from our brand's campaign minus sales losses to competitive brands advertised during the gaps in our brand's schedule. Because such gaps are normally inevitable, the medium-term effect of advertising is virtually always smaller that the short-term effect. The size of the medium-term effect is determined not only by the creative content of the campaign, but also by the brand's budget and its media strategy. Sales promotions can add to the effect of advertising; such synergy is strongest when promotions coincide with the most powerful advertising campaigns.

Brands grow for at least eight reasons:

1. The quality and substance of the creative element in the advertising: generally the most important single factor influencing a brand's progress.
2. The size of the advertising budget.
3. The continuity provided by the brand's media schedule
4. The number and value of consumer promotions. These are normally devices to reduce temporarily the consumer price of the brand, coupons being the most prevalent type of promotion used in the United States.
5. The number and value of trade promotions, all of which are price-related and, in effect, discounts to the retail trade. Trade promotions, although they cost a manufacturer much more money than either media advertising or consumer promotions, have little direct effect on the consumer.[1] Such consumer effects as they have are felt through (a) extending the range of a brand's retail distribution; (b) increasing display at point of sale; (c) the occasions on which a manufacturer's brand appears in the retailer's own advertising; and (d) strengthening a consumer promotion by the retailer doubling or tripling the face value of a manufacturer's coupon.
6. A significant improvement in the functional efficiency of the brand itself.

7. Favorable publicity and word of mouth about the brand because it has in some way become a source of news.
8. Troubles afflicting the brand's competitors.

Brands decline for similar reasons, and here competition takes first place in importance. We must regard our brand from the point of view of the competition. Our strengths become their weaknesses, and vice versa. All the reasons listed above will now apply to competitive brands and will thus impinge unfavorably upon our own brand.

By far the most important factors are Numbers 1, 2, 3, and 4 on the list. Number 1—the quality of the advertising—invariably embraces Number 6, significant improvements in a brand's functional efficiency. In fact, Number 6 is part of Number 1, because a functional improvement will be the basis of a brand restage or relaunch, and the announcement of the improvement becomes the most important task for the advertising. If it is not communicated speedily and efficiently, its value will be catastrophically reduced. My own experience of this type of failure comes from laundry detergents, a field in which it is particularly difficult to interest homemakers in product innovation.

This chapter is concerned with Numbers 1, 2, and 4: the content of the campaign, the size of the advertising investment, and the amount of consumer promotion. Number 3, media continuity, will be discussed in Chapter 5. I shall be examining these marketing inputs with the use of data from the seventy-eight advertised brands from my original pure single-source study of American Nielsen data. Readers should remember the solid statistical basis of this work. It was derived from a total of more than 110,000 statistical calculations, or an average of 1,400 readings per brand. The research therefore stands up to a substantial degree of generalization.

In this chapter the data will be analyzed in three ways. First, I shall test the predictive capacity of the gatekeeper, which was described in Chapter 3 as the device to screen brands that should receive further investment, separating them from those that should not. Second, I shall look at the three inputs—STAS, advertising intensity, and promotional intensity—separately and in combination. And third, I shall examine the thirty-nine brands that increased their shares over the course of the first year of the research and attempt to tease out the relative importance of the causes of that growth. A separate section on sales promotions is inserted between the second and third points above.

Testing the Gatekeeper

Readers will remember from Chapter 3 that a STAS differential of 120 or more should permit a brand to pass through the gate and qualify for further investment. Also allowed through should be those brands with a STAS differential in the marginal 105 to 119 range but which command a significantly above-average consumer price. With the latter brands, it can be realistically assumed that the advertising is justifying to consumers a higher-than-average price, in addition to boosting volume to a modest degree. These two groups provided respectively thirty-one and seven different brands, or a total of thirty-eight.

We can plot the progress of these brands. We can also review the progress of the forty brands that did not pass through the gate and whose campaigns would normally have been stopped while fresh advertising was being developed. The gatekeeper was a hypothetical concept as it related to my original seventy-eight brands. But the analysis of the sales progress of these brands enables the hypothetical gatekeeper to be transformed into an operational tool for the management of advertising. This analysis was made in the following way.

For all the brands, I made four separate calculations—all based on the brand's competitive position—and averaged the brands in each group:

- *Growth*. This is based on market share, to measure the brand in relation to its competitors. It specifically shows the brand's average share during the last nine months of the year in comparison with its share during the first three months. It thus demonstrates progress through the year itself: an ongoing measure of the brand's success or failure in the medium term.
- *STAS differential*. This measures the endemic strength of the campaign.[2]
- *Advertising intensity*. This examines the media budget put behind the campaign and expresses the advertising investment *relative to the size of the brand*. Two brands of the same size can have greatly different advertising budgets (measured as two different advertising intensities), but even a large budget for a small brand will generally be smaller than the budget for a large brand.[3] It is however important to compare like with like: small with small and large with large.
- *Promotional intensity*. This measures the brand's expenditure on consumer promotions relative to the competition.[4]

Table 4.1

Brands That Pass, and Do Not Pass, Through the Gate

	Number brands	Average growth index	Average STAS differential index	Average advertising intensity index	Average promotion intensity index
Brands that pass through the gate	38	113	153	2.3	109
Brands that do not pass through the gate	40	100	96	2.3	110

The results of this analysis are shown in Table 4.1. The meaning of Table 4.1 is totally clear. The brands that pass through the gate grew by 13 percent. This is a very substantial increase for brands in highly competitive product categories that show no aggregate growth, as was the case with the seventy-eight brands analyzed. The forty brands that should not have passed through the gate showed no growth at all.

The average STAS differential shows a large gap between the brands that pass through the gate and those that do not. There is no difference at all between the two groups in advertising intensity and in promotional intensity.

The difference between the two groups can therefore be robustly explained by the STAS differential, a measure of the innate strength of the advertising campaign. The gatekeeper was formulated to be a measure of this campaign strength, and it is predictive. The gatekeeper effectively guards the gate. This conclusion is unambiguous. But it conceals certain internal relationships between the inputs. These are examined by the methods described in the next section.

Three Inputs and How They Operate Together

Table 4.2 examines brand growth. It is a matrix relating two influences on brand growth: STAS differential and advertising intensity. With both of these I have split the data into two groups: (a) average and above and (b) below average. The average STAS differential was 124, with twenty-four brands being average or above, and fifty-four below. The average advertising intensity was 2.3.

Table 4.2 demonstrates a number of interesting points:

Table 4.2

Matrix Relating STAS Differential to Advertising Intensity

	Advertising intensity below average	Advertising intensity average and above	Total
STAS differential average and above	13 brands average growth index 112	11 brands average growth index 135	24 brands average growth index 122
STAS differential below average	36 brands average growth index 96	18 brands average growth index 104	54 brands average growth index 99

- The twenty-four brands with the top STAS measures (average and above) grew by 22 percent.
- The fifty-four brands with the below-average STAS measures showed no growth.
- Of the twenty-four brands with the top STAS measures, only eleven combined their high STAS with high advertising intensity, and these achieved an average growth of 35 percent, which is spectacular in the field of repeat-purchase packaged goods.
- With the brands that generated a below-average STAS differential, high-advertising intensity makes little difference to their performance. In sales terms, the brands with heavy advertising were 4 percent in the black (104); those without it were 4 percent in the red (96). Extra repetition has very little influence on a basically ineffective campaign.

The two important points revealed so far—the key importance of STAS as gatekeeper and the role of the media budget in prolonging sales growth by engineering a repeated short-term effect—support the proposition that *the short-term effect of an advertisement determines whether or not that advertisement will have a medium-term effect.* A repetition of short-term effects over a period (normally twelve months)—effects felt exclusively during the periods when the brand is advertised—adds up to a medium-term effect.

The STAS differential and advertising intensity are of course natural

Table 4.3

Matrix Relating Advertising Effort to Promotional Intensity

	Promotional intensity below average	Promotional intensity average and above	Total
Advertising effort average and above	12 brands average growth index 111	13 brands average growth index 132	25 brands average growth index 122
Advertising effort below average	32 brands average growth index 96	21 brands average growth index 101	53 brands average growth index 98

partners. They work together for the simple reason that advertising intensity determines (in conjunction with the brand's media strategy, discussed in Chapter 5) whether or not the advertising will be exposed often enough to prolong the short-term effect of the campaign over a longer period.

The two measures should therefore be knitted together, quantity being added to quality. This can be done quite simply, by multiplying the STAS differential index for each brand by its advertising intensity. The resulting calculation is called the index of advertising effort.[5] (Figures for individual quintiles will be found in Table 4.5 on page 47.)

The analysis in Table 4.3 is in the form of another matrix: this time relating advertising effort to promotional intensity. The average figure for advertising effort is 283; twenty-five brands exceeded this average and fifty-three were below it. The average promotional intensity was 110.

The conclusions from Table 4.3 are striking:

- Medium-term growth is exclusively associated with above-average advertising effort (22 percent growth for the twenty-five high-advertising-effort brands, compared with no growth for the fifty-three brands whose advertising effort was low).
- Among the brands with above-average advertising effort, promotional intensity provides a significant extra stimulus to sales (132 compared with 111).
- With low advertising effort, promotional intensity, whether high or low, makes little difference to a brand's progress.

This analysis generates an important concept. At the higher levels of advertising effort, sales promotions work synergistically to boost the already high influence of the advertising. In other words, sales promotions can add to the effect of advertising; such synergy is strongest when promotions coincide with the most powerful advertising campaigns. This is a topic important enough to be examined separately and in a little detail.

Sales Promotions: Their Upside and Downside

Sales promotions directed at the consumer account for about a quarter of large consumer goods companies' combined advertising plus promotional budgets. Trade promotions account for another 50 percent and consumer advertising for the remaining quarter.[6] As hinted earlier in this chapter, trade promotions do not have an influence on the consumer commensurate to their cost to manufacturers, and they will not be discussed here. However, consumer promotions—as the name implies—are aimed at the consumer, although not totally because they also have an indirect effect on the retail trade by boosting distribution and encouraging in-store display.

Consumer promotions that, like trade promotions, are really discounts—a euphemism for a reduction in revenue—have five important characteristics. Two are positive and two are very negative. (One is neutral and is a description of reality.) Consumer promotions are mostly variants on the theme of offering lower prices to the consumer, for example, coupons, reduced price packs, banded packs (four for the price of three). We can generalize about the effect of price reduction on consumer purchases. Based on published averages of typical cases, the effect on purchasing of a given percentage reduction in consumer price is almost nine times as large as the effect of the same percentage increase in advertising expenditure.[7] The immediate and powerful effect of consumer promotions makes them dangerously attractive to manufacturers.

The word "dangerously" is used deliberately. This is because of the second characteristic of promotions, both those directed at the consumer and at the trade. The extra sales volume increases direct costs, such as those for raw material and packaging, which generally represent a high proportion of a manufacturer's total expenses. This increase in costs, allied to the reduction in revenue from the promotion (which could be 10 percent or more), will generally pinch out the brand's profitability. This means that a typical brand will earn less from the larger volume sold on deal than from the smaller volume sold at normal prices.

Figure 4.1   **Week-by-Week Sales, Consumer Price, and Advertising, Brand XAA** (indexed figures)

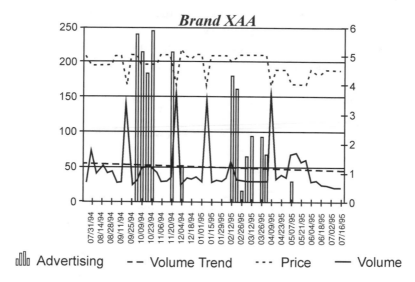

The third characteristic of promotions is that they have a mostly finite effect. The boost to sales generally stops when the promotion stops. This fact has been known for decades.[8] Sometimes promotions are followed by an actual reduction in sales because they will have brought forward future sales that would have been made at full prices. The A.C. Nielsen company calls this the "mortgaging" effect of promotions.

The extremely short-term nature of promotional sales increases is illustrated in Figure 4.1, which shows the weekly sales pattern of a typical brand, code named XAA. The large but temporary response of sales to price cuts can be seen in all four instances in which the price was reduced. Note that *the volume sales trend for this brand is downward*, which means that the price-cutting had the opposite of a positive long-term effect.

The fourth point explains why manufacturers continue to pursue a sales strategy so apparently self-destructive as sales promotions. Manufacturers are forced into it by double pressure: from both the retail trade and their competitors in the market place. Promotions are a cost of doing business with the retail store chains, whose executives know perfectly well that one manufacturer can be played off against another to bid up promotional discounting. Promotions are therefore inevitable,

Figure 4.2 **Week-by-Week Sales, Consumer Price, and Advertising, Brand YAA** (indexed figures)

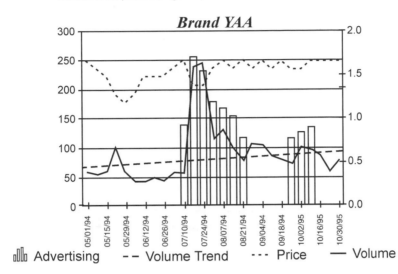

ıllı Advertising   − − Volume Trend   · · · Price   — Volume

and the best that manufacturers can do is to maximize any benefits promotions can provide.

For a start, additional sales volume makes an increased contribution to the general overhead, despite the loss of profit from the individual brand. But there can be an additional compensation, which is the fifth (and quite positive) point about consumer promotions. They can quite often work hand in glove with consumer advertising to nudge a brand's sales trend upward. There is a limited amount of aggregated evidence that this type of synergy can take place in about half of all cases.[9] It should be emphasized that such synergy does not call for advertising that features the promotion. The normal "theme" advertising serves. But it is important that both activities should take place *at the same time,* so that the consumer will be stimulated from two different directions simultaneously.

This point is illustrated in Figure 4.2, which shows how, for Brand YAA, advertising and promotion were planned to coincide, with the result that we see a rising sales trend across the months illustrated in the diagram. Such joint planning of advertising and promotions is still relatively rare, despite all the debate surrounding the doctrine of integrated marketing communications. Much more commonly, advertising and promotions are planned separately and sometimes kept deliberately apart in order to prolong the number of weeks when there is at least some

Table 4.4

Growing Brands: Medium-Term Growth Compared With Individual Marketing Stimuli

Growing quintile	Growth index	STAS differential reindexed	Advertising intensity reindexed	Promotional intensity reindexed
Top	209	134	217	109
Fourth	139	102	238	82
Third	130	90	150	95
Second	125	98	111	110
Bottom	120	96	78	95
Baseline—average of declining brands	100	100	100	100

marketing support behind a brand. As can be seen in Figure 4.1, such separation cuts off all possibility of synergy for Brand XAA.

The cooperation that can take place between advertising and consumer promotions is especially fruitful with those advertising campaigns that are qualitatively and quantitatively the strongest. This point will be discussed in the concluding section of this chapter.

Growing Brands and Why They Grow

We now concentrate on the thirty-nine brands that show medium-term growth. These form the top five deciles of the whole range of seventy-eight brands shown in Table 2.2. in Chapter 2. I have taken the average growth of the five bottom deciles—the declining brands—and indexed this average as 100. This provides the base from which the increases in the growing brands can be measured. The data relating to each of the deciles of growing brands—those describing the growth and also the three main marketing inputs—are indexed on this base. Since there are five growing deciles, these will now be more correctly labeled as the five growing quintiles. (A quintile is a unit of one-fifth, compared to a decile, a unit of one-tenth.)

Table 4.4 compares the growth in each quintile with the equivalent figure for each stimulus separately—STAS differential, advertising intensity, and promotional intensity. With this analysis none of the three separate stimuli is an accurate predictor of growth. The least efficient of them is promotional intensity, which confirms the point made in this chapter that promotions have no effect beyond the short term.

Table 4.5

Growing Brands: Medium-Term Growth Compared With Advertising Effort (STAS differential multiplied by advertising intensity)

Growing quintile	Growth index	Advertising effort Iindex
Top	209	260
Fourth	139	199
Third	130	139
Second	125	105
Bottom	120	79
Baseline—average of all declining brands	100	100

Figure 4.3   **Quintile Analysis of Thirty-nine Brands Showing Medium-Term Growth** (indexed on thirty-nine declining brands [= 100])

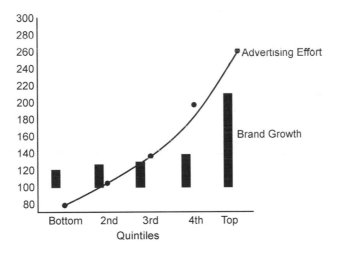

We get much more promising results when we combine the stimuli, by looking at the relationship between growth and advertising effort. This is shown in Table 4.5 and plotted in Figure 4.3. The effects can be seen most dramatically in the diagram. The trajectory of the advertising curve is more pronounced than the final out-turn in brand growth. The advertising input figures start lower and end higher. But there is no break in the series, and it can be seen that the fit of the curve is good. There is actually some advantage in producing input curves that are steeper than the out-turn, because the operational lessons from the analysis become clearer.

Table 4.6

Medium-Term Growth Compared With Combined Marketing Inputs for Four Successful Brands

Category	Breakfast cereal	Liquid detergent	Bar soap	Packaged detergent
STAS differential	121	133	193	253
Advertising intensity	2.2	5.0	2.0	3.5
Promotional intensity	70	108	122	163
Advertising effort	266	665	386	886
Medium-term growth (percent)	+22	+25	+78	+119

This analysis is made with the aim of helping advertisers boost their brands in large, competitive, and often stagnant markets. Here are four guidelines.

- The competitive functional performance of their brands must be good enough to support advertising investment. In the eyes of consumers, the brand must justify repurchase.
- Manufacturers should make sure that their brand's advertising generates a high STAS differential. If not, they must persist until they produce a campaign that does; otherwise the campaign should not be allowed through the gate.
- A brand's budget will inevitably be governed by its present and/or anticipated profitability. Within these limits, above-average investment is strongly recommended for those campaigns that generate a high STAS differential. This will certainly be the case for new brands, which must invest at a high level in order to get established.
- It is less desirable to boost consumer promotions in view of their uneconomic cost. However, pressures in the market place will force manufacturers to promote, and when this happens there is merit in concentrating the promotional support on those brands with a high STAS differential plus high-advertising intensity. In all events, advertising and promotions should *coincide in time* in order to maximize synergy.

Consider the four examples in Table 4.6, which are of course real brands. These appear in ascending order of sales effect (reading left to right). Note in particular the fundamental importance of the STAS differential and how advertising intensity reinforces its effect.

In summary, this chapter has described four phenomena from which it is possible to draw operational lessons.

First, the STAS differential guards the gate. It should control whether or not an advertising campaign justifies further investment.

Second, the range of medium-term effects is less pronounced than the range of STAS differentials. This demonstrates that over time the STAS effect erodes as a result of competitive activity in the market place.

Third, in order to minimize this erosion, an advertiser should support a campaign that achieves a high STAS differential with the highest affordable advertising intensity. Consumer promotions should be timed to support the advertising, and within a general policy of using promotions sparingly, they should be used for brands that have effective advertising, rather than to compensate for ineffective advertising.

Fourth, the index of advertising effort can be used to predict in crude terms the sales growth of successful brands.

Are the lessons in this chapter a shadow of the holy grail of advertising? We cannot make any such claim until a model has been constructed that includes an evaluation of advertising's long-term effect. This is not the concern of this book. But we must here consider the tactical application of above-average advertising intensity and discuss how this can be used to build advertising continuity, which (as explained at the beginning of this chapter) is one of the eight determinants of the growth of a brand.

Notes

1. This information comes from research among a sample of large advertisers contacted regularly by Cox Communications. John Philip Jones, "Trends in Promotions," in *The Advertising Business: Operations, Creativity, Media Planning, Integrated Communications,* ed. John Philip Jones, pp. 321–324 (Thousand Oaks, CA: Sage Publications, 1999).

2. As explained in Chapter 2, the STAS differential measures the difference in a brand's market share between its ad households and adless households. The former receive advertising for the brand during the seven days before the brand is bought; the latter do not.

3. Advertising intensity is a measure of the size of the brand's advertising media budget in relation to that of its competitors in the same product category. It is based on the brand's share of voice, for example, its share of all advertising in the category. Advertising intensity is the ratio of a brand's share of voice to its share of market; for example, if advertising intensity is 2.0, then the brand's advertising share is twice as high as its market share—say, 6 percent compared with 3 percent. For most brands, share of voice is larger than share of market, because there are always some unadvertised brands in all categories. Therefore, the average share of voice will be larger than share of market, because the latter is based on *all* brands while share of voice is derived from the advertised brands alone; for the unadvertised brands it will be zero.

4. Promotional intensity is also based on competitive activity within a brand's product category. It is measured by the percentage of the brand's volume sold on deal, for example, at a special, reduced price, compared with the category average (indexed at 100).

5. I have chosen the simplest way of making the calculation. It does not matter precisely how the sums are carried out so long as the same method is used consistently in all cases. The purpose of this piece of arithmetic is simply to make *comparisons between brands* on the basis of their relative advertising effort. Alternative systems of calculating the advertising effort would put different brands in the same relationship to each other although the numbers might be different.

6. See n. 1.

7. These averages are based on substantial numbers of cases. See Gert Assmus, John U. Farlet, and Donald R. Lehmann, "How Advertising Affects Sales: A Meta-Analysis of Econometric Results," *Journal of Marketing Research*, February 1984, pp. 65–74. Also Gerard J. Tellis, "The Price Elasticity of Selective Demand: A Meta-Analysis of Econometric Models of Sales," *Journal of Marketing Research*, November 1988, pp. 331–341. Also John Philip Jones, "The Double Jeopardy of Sales Promotions," *Harvard Business Review*, September–October 1990, pp. 145–152.

8. James O. Peckham Sr., *The Wheel of Marketing,* 2nd ed. (privately published, 1981, but available from A.C. Nielsen), pp. 52–70.

9. Abbas Bendali, "Do Promotions Need Media Support?" *Commercial Communications: The Journal of Advertising and Marketing Policy and Practice in the European Community*, January 1997, pp. 13–16.

— 5 —

Keeping the Brand in the Window

Erwin Ephron, a New York media consultant who combines a researcher's understanding of principles and underlying causes with pragmatic knowledge derived from a lifetime of practical experience of media planning and buying for major brands, once used this striking metaphor: "Visualize a window of advertising opportunity in front of each purchase. Advertising's job is to influence that purchase. Recency planning's job is to place the message in that window."[1]

This chapter is devoted to the concept of recency. This embraces two things: continuity and propinquity. Continuity means planning the advertising to appear "in the window" for as many weeks over the course of a year as the budget will permit. Propinquity means ensuring that the advertising message appears near the time when the buyer experiences an impulse to buy one or another brand in the category. The decision to buy a *product* (irrespective of the particular brand chosen) is generally uninfluenced by advertising. It is governed, in the case of packaged goods, by whether the last box in the home has been used up, and in other fields it happens when the need arises. However, there is no doubt at all that advertising can influence the choice of *brand* for the replacement purchase, and it does this generally by reminding, which means evoking prior brand experience. This is a more realistic description of the process than the rational phrase "influencing a decision."

The Buying Process

The buying process for all consumer goods is more turbulent than non-specialist observers imagine. The purchasing of brands by individual consumers is complicated (as we shall shortly see). And the aggregate purchasing in a market, made up as it is by the purchases of millions of consumers buying a multiplicity of brands with great regularity, introduces an exponential degree of further complication, which means we need a research technique as data-intensive as pure single-source in order to dig out the effects of advertising.

Advertising is quite capable of influencing sales, as we saw in Chapters 2, 3, and 4. But to explain more fully how an immediate short-term effect can be prolonged into the medium term, I must start by making three general points about consumer purchasing.

First, in the majority of categories, consumers buy repeatedly. With day-to-day purchases, such as extremely inexpensive ones like individual telephone calls or e-mails, the repetition takes place with great regularity within an extremely short period. At the other end of the range are durables like cars, which consumers buy regularly but where the repurchase period is extended over years. Goods sold in food and drugstores come between the two extremes, with the repetition interval usually of one to four weeks. The latter products account for the most household expenditure and are the main concern of this chapter.

The second characteristic of purchasing is that in the majority of categories, most buyers are women, for the simple reason that homemakers tend to be female. Social evolution—in particular, change in the roles of the sexes—brings about a diminishing proportion of female buyers, but women homemakers are still prevalent enough for me to adopt the widespread convention of calling buyers "she" and not "he." Housewives have a good relationship with their brands, but the sheer number of different brand purchases they make in all the product fields they buy reaches in most cases more than a thousand in a year. It follows that the individual decision to choose one brand over another is not too serious a matter. It is rarely planned beforehand and equally rarely subject to post hoc examination. The process has been described as "low involvement."

The third point, and the one that is most relevant to the role of advertising, is that buyers buy a number of different brands, and it is fairly rare for more than 20 percent of purchasing in any category over the course of a year to be made by buyers of one brand only (a group known technically as solus buyers).[2] The group of brands bought by a consumer is described as her brand repertoire.

Here is a typical example of one homemaker's purchases in one heavily bought category over a two-year period. The brand names are coded by letters of the alphabet:[3] BOODGBOCOBGBGABBGBBDBGBCBBGGBBB. This consumer "shows a trend toward brand B and a cycle in buying brand G which recurs on average 4.4 times."[4] Over the period, this housewife made thirty-one separate product purchases, and she had a repertoire of six different brands. She bought brand B fifteen times; G, seven times; O, four times; C twice; D twice; and A once. This pattern is typical. Most buyers have a favorite brand (B), a second favorite (G), and a rotating third brand (either O, C, D, or A in this example).

The importance of this analysis to an advertiser is that his buyers will be using and comparing both his own and his competitors' brands. These buyers will therefore be appropriate targets for his and his competitors' advertising. And since the buyers use all these brands either regularly or intermittently, they will be modestly inclined to pay attention to these brands' advertising because of selective perception. Consumers tend to look, or at least half-look, at the advertising for the brands they use.

With repeat-purchase package goods, household purchasing tends to take place weekly, generally on Thursday, Friday, or Saturday. But much buying takes place on other days as well. If we add together the buying of all the consumers in any product category—many millions of people in most cases—it is easy to visualize the massive amount of buying that takes place every day, with an even larger amount toward the end of the week. People buy when their household stocks are low or depleted. Each household has a purchase interval for its brands: the period between purchases maybe three weeks for toothpaste or one week for breakfast cereals. But repurchase takes place on different days in different weeks for different households. And people who buy one brand today will possibly or even probably buy a different brand next time.

There are huge numbers of potential buyers at all times for all established brands in every category. And in every category, the pattern of buying shows a constant interchange of brand shares, the "ups" for a specific brand reflecting its advertising at the time: provided, of course, that the campaign has a positive short-term advertising strength (STAS). If only one brand it advertised, this will directly attract customers from all others. If more than one is advertised at the same time, the brand

Figure 5.1   **Schematic Diagram of Sales Gains and Losses for Brand AAA Over the Course of a Year**

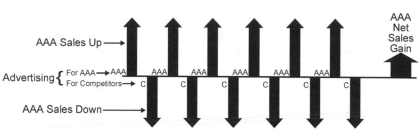

whose campaign generates the highest STAS differential will do best. The gaps in a brand's schedule will therefore cause losses of business because millions of potential buyers have been missed. This process is illustrated in Figure 5.1, a hypothetical picture, although the lesson it contains is real enough. Each short-term sales increase represents the size of the STAS differential. The net gain at the end of the year represents the sum of short-term gains minus the sum of short-term losses. The sales increases for brand AAA are due to the advertising for AAA, and the losses stem from the advertising for competitive brands.

The end result is as we see in Figure 5.2, which describes a real German brand, ZAA, whose STAS differential index (B minus A) showed a rise of 50 percent, but whose medium-term sales improvement (D minus C) was only 14 percent. The difference between the two numbers was the result of the gaps in ZAA's schedule, when consumers were responding to the advertising for competitive brands.

The performance of brand ZAA, despite the drop from 50 percent to 14 percent, is actually good. The losses of business below the STAS differential are greater for most other brands. In many cases the effect of a positive STAS completely disappears as a result of the stronger and more continuously exposed campaigns for competitive brands, which means that the brands will lose their STAS and end the year in negative territory.

In view of the vigorous forces of competition, it is obvious that if advertising for a brand is to be placed "in the window" in order to be seen by the countless numbers of people who are in the market, then it must have a permanent advertising presence, or at least as permanent a presence as the budget will allow. Advertising presence naturally means *effective* presence, reaching a large enough number of consumers every week to influence the total volume of sales. Also, advertising should

Figure 5.2   **STAS Differential and Medium-Term Sales Effect for Brand ZAA**

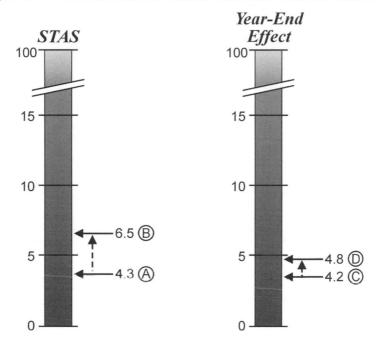

appear immediately before the buying takes place, when it has the greatest effect (as we shall see). This is the meaning of propinquity.

This then is the basic rationale for the strategy of recency: (1) Large amounts of buying take place weekly; media should therefore be planned weekly. Since the advertising is required to influence the buying, the weekly reach must be sufficiently large for an effect in the market place. Advertisers should aim for a minimal effective coverage of targeted homes, but without extravagance. (2) Buying tends to take place toward the end of the week; media should therefore be planned similarly. (3) Buying never stops; media exposure should therefore never stop, or stop only when it is restricted by the budget.

When this doctrine was first propagated, it upset many deeply rooted beliefs. Indeed, the importance of continuity, in particular, is still not universally accepted, although the skeptics now represent a diminishing minority. But in addition to the doubts of these most conservative practitioners, there are two factors that inhibit the ability to achieve continuity. The first is the size of the budget. Most manufacturers simply cannot afford to advertise all year round, and this represents a permanent prob-

Figure 5.3   **Advertising Response Function With Threshold**
(S-shaped curve)

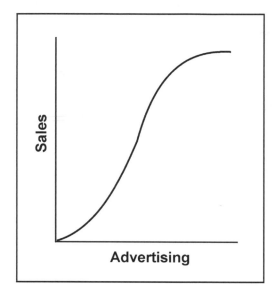

lem. In the real world, the budget for an ongoing (as opposed to a new) brand is governed inevitably by its profitability. It is unrealistic to expect manufacturers to accept advice to spend more money and thereby sacrifice immediate profit, no matter what benefits greater media continuity can offer in the longer term.

Despite a rather subtle but important relationship between the size of a brand and the size of its advertising budget—a relationship that can yield scale economies for larger brands[5]—the size of the media budget will not be discussed in this present context. I shall take the media budget as given, saying only that a successful market place outcome from recency planning will probably lead to increased budgets in the long term as the brand grows. Advertisers must concern themselves with the most effective deployment of existing media dollars. This brings me to the second problem with the application of continuity.

This problem is caused by the extent to which traditional patterns of media buying unconsciously build waste into media plans, thus misusing resources that could be used to provide continuity. To evaluate this second point, we must examine a technical matter, the shape of the advertising response function.

Figure 5.4   **Advertising Response Function Without Threshold**
(concave-downward curve)

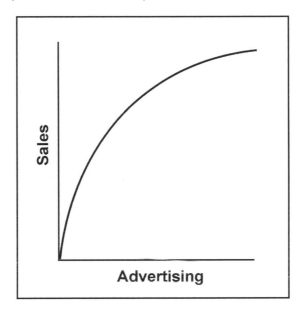

The Advertising Response Function

The response function is an example of a theory with a directly practical application. It describes the amount of advertising needed to trigger buying. In particular, it illustrates the sales effect of additional amounts of advertising and whether they generate increments of sales at an increasing or diminishing rate. These points will become clearer by comparing Figure 5.3 and Figure 5.4.

In Figures 5.3 and 5.4, the horizontal axis plots equal "doses" of advertising. These can be measured in a number of ways: in dollars, television gross rating points, or consumer impressions ("opportunities-to-see"). The vertical axis plots the *incremental* sales that are generated by the progressive doses of advertising. We see therefore *varying* amounts of sales output that have resulted from *equal* amounts of advertising input.

In Figure 5.3, extra advertising causes sales to increase at a growing rate, building up to a threshold shown by the bend in the curve (known as the inflexion point), where the increasing sales increments change to diminishing ones. The amount of advertising that produces the greatest sales effect for the advertising dollar is measured at the inflexion point, where the marginal—or additional—dose of advertising produces greatest return.

In Figure 5.4, all doses of advertising produce sales results, but the increments decline from the beginning. The first advertising generates the most sales; the second produces extra volume, but less than the first; the third produces more still, but less than the second. Hence, diminishing returns.

Two Response Functions: Two Strategies

These alternative theories are used to support two different ways of deploying advertising money. Figure 5.3 underpins a once popular belief that a fixed number of advertisement exposures (generally considered to be three) have to be received by the consumer before the advertising will seriously influence her purchasing behavior. This number of exposures was considered to be the threshold representing maximum effect. The result was the popular policy of compressing the advertising into confined periods to obtain an effective frequency of three.

With the alternative theory of diminishing returns shown in Figure 5.4, the first dose of advertising is seen to be the most productive one, and extra doses produce increases that become progressively smaller. These are less economic because each diminishing sales increment costs the same advertising budget as the one before. The way to exploit diminishing returns is to create during each week a strong effect by covering a large audience *once* and no more. The advertiser can then move on to the next week, when the advertising can be used to stimulate fresh sales, again with one strong exposure. This is a broad description of continuity planning.

As I have suggested, the theory embodied in Figure 5.3 once received wide support. This meant that the advertising schedules of the majority of brands in most countries around the world were for many decades made up of two- or three- or four-week periods of advertising, each concentrated to achieve effective frequency. These periods were separated by intervals during which there was no advertising. The gaps were, of course, unavoidable because advertising budgets could not run to year-round exposure at a heavy rate. The pockets of concentration in such schedules are known as flights in the United States and as bursts in Europe.[6]

Until the 1990s the shape of the advertising response function was not a subject of great interest to the advertising business. As I have said, the majority of media plans employed flights, a policy that was tacitly based on the S-shaped response function shown in Figure 5.3. It was unlikely that media planners, who are practical people, were much concerned with the theoretical basis of the strategy of media concentration that was automatically—and perhaps unthinkingly—applied in virtually all circumstances.

The influential research study *Effective Frequency: The Relationship Between Frequency and Advertising Effectiveness*, sponsored by the Advertising Research Foundation and published by the Association of National Advertisers in 1979, gave academic support to a flighting strategy.[7] The main piece of evidence in this book came from Colin McDonald's pilot study carried out in Britain in 1966 (described in Chapter 1). This showed an S-shaped curve of a very extreme type, with a single exposure causing a sales *reduction.* Unfortunately this was a result of the way in which McDonald analyzed the data. He used an incomplete method because he measured the response of purchasing to increments of advertising solely by the amount of switching from brand to brand. This method tells only half the story since it ignores repeated purchase of the same brand, which can be influenced by advertising just as much as brand switching can. (See Appendix B.)

I used a more straightforward method of analyzing all the data from the first large-scale piece of pure single-source research in the United States. I measured the change in purchasing caused by advertising—both in absolute and in incremental terms—by a simple change in market share. This struck me at the time as the common-sense approach, and my method has not been disputed since my work was first published in 1995. When McDonald recomputed his 1966 figures using my simpler method, his findings echoed mine—a straightforward pattern of diminishing returns. McDonald's results can be seen in Figure 5.5,[8] mine in Figure 5.6.

My research was planned to measure the sales response to any amount of advertising for a brand during the seven days before it was bought. It was, however, reasonably simple to isolate the sales response in the homes that had received a single advertisement. As can be seen in Figure 5.6, the average share of market for all seventy-eight brands was 7.6 percent in the adless households: the level of the baseline. The share in the ad households that had received only one advertisement was 8.4 percent; in the ad households that had received any number of advertisements, it was 8.7 percent.

My research demonstrated a sharp pattern of diminishing returns, with

Figure 5.5   **Response Function: McDonald's 1966 British Pure Single-Source**
(data recomputed by the Jones Method)

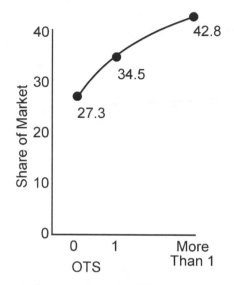

Note: OTS = Opportunity-to-see (i.e., advertising exposure).

73 percent of the short-term business generated by a brand's advertising accounted for by households that had received a single advertisement (0.8 percentage points as a percentage of 1.1 percentage points). An additional 27 percent came from households in which a larger volume of advertising for the brand had appeared on their television screens. My finding, of a 73:27 ratio between the effect of one exposure and subsequent exposures, had some remarkable effects on American advertising practice. The research was also replicated and the subsequent studies have confirmed broadly what I had found.

The first repeat of my American research was in Germany.[9] This showed quite clearly that a single advertisement can be effective—often highly effective. This conclusion has also been confirmed by other American data, from, among others, Lawrence Gibson, and by British data both from Andrew Roberts and from Colin McDonald's large scale Adlab study.[10] McDonald makes an important point by emphasizing propinquity. The greatest sales effect comes from advertising one day before purchase. Fewer sales come from advertising two days before, and fewer still from three days before.[11] McDonald had found the same thing in his 1966 investigation.

Figure 5.6   **Response Function: Nielsen 1991 American Pure Single-Source** (data from seventy-eight brands)

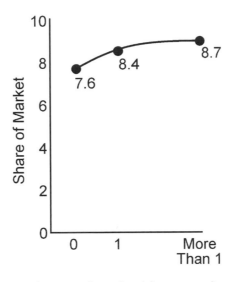

Note: OTS = Opportunity-to-see (i.e., advertising exposure).

My count of published response functions shows more than 200 brands whose campaigns show diminishing returns, and slightly more than ten— mainly new brands —whose campaigns show S-shaped thresholds. The logic of media concentration, on at least a temporary basis, for new brands is that new product concepts and new advertising campaigns need a degree of repetition before consumers can understand them. Otherwise, researchers accept diminishing returns and media planners accept continuity.

Diminishing Returns in Europe

There is a special point that is worth making about the difference between my findings from the United States and those from Germany. This illustrates dramatically the waste involved in concentrating advertising money in ignorance of the vicious effect of diminishing returns. The normal reduction in advertising efficiency caused by diminishing returns will effectively cause a large difference between an immediate sales lift from STAS and a year-end sales increase. As I have mentioned, it is common to find a positive immediate effect ending up in a year-end sales *reduction*.

Table 5.1

STAS Minus Year-End Sales Change (in percent)

Decile	United States (high falloff)	Germany (low falloff)
First	−54	−16
Second	−43	−7
Third	−26	−1
Fourth	−12	No difference
Fifth	−13	No difference
Sixth	−10	No difference
Seventh	−9	−4
Eighth	−7	−5
Ninth	−5	−3
Tenth	−4	−1

In the United States, I found a very sharp pattern of diminishing returns in the advertising response function: as explained, an average 73:27 ratio of effects from one exposure to further exposures. Media concentration—which swallows large amounts of money—causes the average advertising budget to run down very fast, and the loss of potential sales caused by the diminishing returns means that any short-term sales gain simply cannot be maintained across a year. Table 5.1 examines the falloff of short-term effects by the end of the year. All the brands from my American study are ranked in deciles from the campaigns with the strongest STAS (first decile) to the weakest (tenth decile). The inefficiency of concentrated scheduling is amply illustrated by the consistent dissipation of the short-term effects.

The situation in Germany is different. Here the rate of diminishing returns is much less sharp than in the United States, with a sales effect from the first exposure compared with additional exposures in the ratio of 46:54. Additional exposures beyond one are still generating a good deal of business. In Germany, therefore, concentrated pressure leads to *less falloff in sales and less decay of the short-term effect* than in the United States.

The difference in the rate of falloff between the two countries is startling, and it emphasizes the terrible loss of potential sales in the United States that concentrated advertising schedules will bring about. Seventy percent of campaigns generate short-term sales increases. Of these, 46 percent maintain higher sales at the end of the year, although the effect was always less than the original STAS. Twenty-four percent (i.e., 70 minus 46) totally lost their positive effect on sales, for reasons connected with media weight and scheduling.

An additional discovery of McDonald's is worth mentioning. Although most sales come from the homes that receive a single advertisement, additional exposures *do* generate some extra business: a very small amount in the United States, but rather more in Europe, where the onset of diminishing returns is less steep. In Europe, it is likely that the buyers who watch an above-average amount of television will receive extra advertisements for a brand. And heavy television viewers in Europe tend to buy more of a brand than do light viewers (because of the number of children in the household). Similarly, light viewers buy less.

McDonald called this effect purchasing/viewing (P/V) bias.[12] It goes both ways, causing European STAS figures to be slightly imprecise.

How we use the data depends on the distribution of heavy and light viewers in the target audience for our brand's media schedule. As a general rule, covering all television viewing in most countries, about 40 percent of homes are heavy viewers (in varying degrees); 20 percent of homes are average viewers; and 40 percent of homes are light viewers (again in varying degrees).

The 60 percent of average and heavy viewers are obviously unaffected by this analysis. Their STAS will be either average or above average. The light viewers are more problematical, although more in theory than in practice. This is because advertisers commonly spend at least 10 percent of their total advertising budgets on general and specialist magazines to reach light television viewers, who are often the better educated and more affluent families. There is therefore a built-in compensation for the likelihood of these consumers generating a below-average STAS from television on its own. They receive additional stimuli from print media.

As mentioned, the P/V bias is a European problem rather than an American one. In the United States, purchasing levels are relatively uniform across the different viewing groups. But it will be remembered from Chapter 3 that, to be on the safe side, I advise that the brands with a STAS differential of under 120 should only be allowed through the gate if there is additional evidence (e.g., premium price) that the advertising is effective.

Recency in the Market Place

The size of the medium-term effect is determined not only by the creative content of the campaign, but also by the budget and the media strategy. Budget and media are devices to engineer the advertising continuity needed to protect the brand from competitive assaults.

The most effective media strategy for a brand can be described simply. However, it is not easy to implement such a strategy, because of the complexities of the media market place.

1. Aim to cover a substantial proportion of the brand's target group once every week with as little duplication as possible. "Substantial proportion" is a judgment call based on the size of the brand, its target group, and knowledge of the effectiveness of defined levels of reach achieved in the past.
2. To attain this minimum reach, determine the optimum number of weekly gross rating points (GRPs) and establish the best types of dayparts and television programs to use in order to minimize audience duplication. These procedures are again judgmental, and they require expert knowledge of the television audience and of the fast-changing field of programming. During recent years, Erwin Ephron has done more than any other analyst to put flesh on these theoretical bones.
3. Run the weekly advertising pattern for as many weeks as the budget will allow. Any inevitable gaps in the schedule should occur during the low season.

My recommendations call for redeploying advertising budgets to achieve a greater continuity than many schedules achieve at present, and of course this means less short-term concentration: an economically favorable outcome because of the way it manages to reduce the effect of diminishing returns. Regional test programs are also a good idea so long as they can be carried out efficiently and economically. These thoughts, which would at one time have been considered highly unorthodox, are not falling on deaf ears, in either the United States or Europe.

In the late 1970s, when I was working at J. Walter Thompson, London, the client and agency commissioned an econometric study of the advertising response function for Andrex, a very powerful brand and market leader in the bathroom tissue category. This response function—although it came in the form of a rather weak regression—seemed to show a pattern of diminishing returns. This was nevertheless good enough to persuade the client and agency to plan and run a pattern of continuous advertising in a number of typical television areas. A careful analysis of sales at the end of a year showed significantly stronger sales in the test areas than in the rest of Britain, which acted as the statistical control.

As a result of this test, the national advertising was changed to a pattern of continuous advertising. This was a very unusual thing for an important national brand. However, it has been acknowledged by both client and agency to have benefited the brand enormously over the years. It did this by maintaining the brand's already high penetration and purchase frequency and indeed by preserving Andrex's comfortable market leadership: J. Walter Thompson believes that "this high level of carry-over and behavior maintenance is in some measure attributable to the disposition of advertising weight within and between sales periods. Andrex has, for many years, disposed advertising weight continuously. It is not clustered in bursts."[13]

Such an unprejudiced, experimental mind-set has also been adopted by many American advertisers: an attitude that must be welcomed by the research community. During the course of 1996, I gradually learned about eight major advertisers, with an aggregate national billing of more than $4 billion, who were seriously experimenting with continuity scheduling on an area basis and in some cases were producing demonstrably positive results.

I possess full details of the media experiments carried out by one of these organizations: an extremely prominent advertiser and a company with nine major marketing divisions whose brands are all household names. In 1995, the average number of weeks of advertising across all these divisions was sixteen, at an average weekly advertising weight of ninety-seven GRPs. As a result of successful experimentation during the course of 1996, eight of the nine divisions adjusted the distribution of their advertising funds. In 1997, the average number of advertised weeks in all nine operating divisions had increased to twenty-two, and the average weekly GRP level had been decreased to eighty-four.[14] The company has taken—after good research and careful deliberation—a measurable step toward recency scheduling. The plans also accommodated a good deal of detailed media innovation aimed at stretching the net reach of the schedules and reducing wasteful duplication.

During the course of 1996, the pace of interest in continuity scheduling increased. By December, 53 percent of major clients and 70 percent of senior media executives in agencies were aware of the research into single-exposure effectiveness and the value of continuous advertising. Similar numbers also claimed to be either implementing or considering

Table 5.2

Relative Effectiveness of TV Schedules Based on Different Combinations of Continuity and Weekly Weight

	Weeks on air	Maximum GRPs per week	Index of sales effectiveness
Low continuity	9	240	61
Medium continuity	22	163	106
High continuity	38	193	132

implementing plans to advertise more continuously than before. Interest was particularly strong among packaged goods and automotive advertisers.[15]

In 1999 the celebrated *AdWorks2* study was released to subscribers and selected extracts were published. This was a cooperative enterprise between Media Marketing Assessment Inc. (now Marketing Management Analytics, or MMA) and Information Resources Inc. (IRI). It was an econometric study of more than 800 brands in 200 separate categories, using sales data from 4,000 grocery, drug, and mass merchandiser stores over the two years 1995 and 1996. This research compared the effectiveness of continuity and flighted media plans and reached an unambiguous conclusion: "Continuity plans are more effective than flighted plans. This supports findings from other studies that point to the importance of recency. Brands that are planning to increase weight should first consider adding weeks instead of adding weight to existing flights. Brands with high levels of GRPs delivered per week should consider shifting some weight across additional weeks."[16]

This conclusion was derived from a special calculation of the relative effectiveness of different schedules, based on the average (indexed at 100) for all television schedules covered by the *AdWorks2* research. The relative effectiveness of three mixes of continuity and weekly weight are as shown in Table 5.2. The greater effectiveness of high-continuity scheduling over low continuity is a manifestation of diminishing returns. The continuity schedule benefits from operating every week on a lower—more productive—part of the advertising response curve. In contrast to this, the low-continuity (concentrated) schedule soon hits diminishing returns.

Another way of expressing this same point is that, if two brands with the same budget, size, media costs, and advertising elasticity choose to raise their GRP support by, say, 20 percent, we would be able to see very different volume returns as a result of different patterns of continuity. With additional weeks but no change in the weekly concentration of GRPs, the extra budget would generate extra sales. But if weekly GRP levels are lifted drastically and weeks on-air not increased, we would consistently and quickly see saturation, and overall television effectiveness would not be improved in line with the budget increase. The extra money would be essentially wasted.

As if to write finis to this debate, the Advertising Research Foundation (ARF), which had sponsored the 1979 *Effective Frequency* study, formally announced at the end of 1997 the termination of its support for the doctrine of three-exposure effective frequency. Using a slightly macabre metaphor, the ARF declared: "We agreed to amputate the rule of thumb. And like any amputation, it was painful."[17]

Notes

1. Erwin Ephron, "A Car Is Like a Box of Frosted Flakes." Advertising Research Foundation and European Society for Marketing and Opinion Research. Worldwide Electronic and Broadcast Research Symposium, San Francisco, California, April 1996.

2. This point is picked up in Chapter 11.

3. John Philip Jones and Jan S. Slater, *What's in a Name? Advertising and the Concept of Brands,* 2nd ed. (Armonk, NY: M.E. Sharpe, 2003), p. 110. This particular analysis is based on the work of Michael Barnes, whose original paper is detailed in *What's in a Name?* p. 134.

4. Ibid.

5. John Philip Jones, *The Ultimate Secrets of Advertising* (Thousand Oaks, CA: Sage Publications, 2002), pp. 124–127.

6. A purely instinctive drive to concentrate media weight was commonplace during the period 1953 to 1980 when I worked as an advertising practitioner.

7. *Effective Frequency: The Relationship Between Frequency and Advertising Effectiveness,* ed. Michael J. Naples (New York: Association of National Advertisers, 1979).

8. Colin McDonald, "The Effective Frequency Debate," *Admap,* February 1995, p. 27.

9. John Philip Jones, *When Ads Work: The German Version* (Frankfurt am Main: Gesamtverband Werbeagenturen GWAeV, 1995), pp. 21–24.

10. Lawrence D. Gibson, "What Can One TV Exposure Do?" *Conference Proceedings of Copy Research Workshop* (New York: Advertising Research Foundation, 1994), p. 16; Andrew Roberts, "What Do We Know About Advertising's Short-Term Effects?" *Admap,* February 1996, pp. 42–45; Colin McDonald, "How Frequently Should You Advertise?" *Admap,* July/August 1996, pp. 22–25.

11. However, Walter Reichel and Leslie Wood's analyses of the American Nielsen database suggest that the short-term effect can be felt to a slight degree from advertising that was received up to *four weeks* before the date of purchase. The importance of this conclusion—if it is generally valid—is that continuous weeks of advertising may be able to generate an effect that increases slightly and progressively as a result of tiny additional effects from past periods. See Walter Reichel and Leslie Wood, "Recency

in Media Planning—Redefined," *Journal of Advertising Research*, July/August 1997, pp. 66–74.

12. Colin McDonald, "Short-Term Advertising Effects: How Confident Can We Be?" *Admap*, June 1997, pp. 36–39.

13. Evelyn Jenkins and Christopher Timms, "The Andrex Story: A Soft, Strong and Very Long-Term Success," in *Advertising Works 4: Papers from the Institute of Practitioners in Advertising (IPA) Advertising Effectiveness Awards*, p. 185 (London: Cassell, 1987). This case study is one of two devoted to Andrex published by the IPA. The second came out in 1993.

14. Private information.

15. *Myers Report* (New York: Myers Report Industry Research, December 16, 1996). The data came from surveys of 711 executives in advertiser companies and 300 in advertising agencies.

16. Marketing Management Analytics Inc. and Information Resources Inc., *AdWorks2: Report of Presentation*, 1999.

17. *Myers Report* (New York: Myers Report Industry Research, November 1997).

—— 6 ——

An Interlude
Successful Advertising Campaigns

Many of the ideas raised in the first five chapters of this book will appear radical to some readers. Chapter 6 will be less so. In this, I have attempted to isolate the creative qualities of the campaigns of the Alpha One brands, based on my observation of them. These qualities are not themselves totally unexpected. Indeed, a review of the wisdom of several generations of advertising gurus shows that these qualities have been widely described and discussed in the past, although we must be selective in separating the wheat from the chaff. The voices in this chapter are not those of consumers, but of respected practitioners who made their reputations by understanding consumers.

The most important objectively measurable characteristic of the Alpha One brands is that their advertising campaigns are unusually effective. In their short- and longer-term ability to generate sales, they can be judged alongside the less successful Alpha Two brands. In the strength of their short-term sales effect, they can be contrasted to many of the Beta brands and all brands in the Gamma group. Because of the importance and the relative rarity of creatively effective advertising—especially campaigns with staying power—such campaigns deserve to be discussed in some detail, despite the real problem that I am not at liberty to identify the names of the brands.

As might be expected, the Alpha One campaigns are all different from each other; the brands themselves cover a wide spectrum. But the campaigns share to a remarkable extent three characteristics. The Alpha One campaigns are intrinsically *likable*. They are *visual* rather than verbal. And they encourage engagement by communicating their promise in terms *relevant to consumers.*

These points are more tactical than strategic: more concerned with the creative idea than with the creative objectives. Nevertheless, since a well-constructed strategy gives direction to the campaign itself, I am fairly certain that the three characteristics all originated in embryo in the brands' strategies and were laid down before the campaigns themselves were written.

There is nothing especially original about these points, but to put them in focus, we should appreciate the features that the campaigns do *not* possess. The Alpha One campaigns are not hard-selling: They do not make strong and direct product claims. There are no "slices of life"; no men in white coats demonstrating products; no happy families; in fact, none of the most widely used—and tiresome—advertising clichés. The campaigns are not didactic and verbal. They are characterized by the relatively small number of words on their sound tracks—well below the normally agreed maximum of sixty to seventy—although this does not detract from the strength of their visual demonstrations. In general, the campaigns are concerned with consumer benefits rather than with product features. But there is a delicate balance here, which I try to describe later in this chapter.

The three distinguishing characteristics of the Alpha One campaigns are all endorsed to a greater or lesser degree by most of the best-known writers on advertising. Therefore, instead of devoting this chapter to statistics, I shall take an approach that is likely to be more interesting to readers. I shall quote the dicta of a number of the most respected experts, although I have been extremely selective in the statements I have chosen to use. The writings of these well-known people cover much more ground than the rather narrow range of aphorisms I am using in this chapter. Many of their extensively propagated and widely believed statements not quoted here will be familiar to readers, perhaps more so than the statements I have specifically selected.

Remember, however, that my starting point was the Alpha One campaigns. The experts I shall quote are able to illuminate the features of these in many interesting ways. Readers can, however, correctly infer that my omissions from the experts' published opinions were done for the good reason that my research could provide no substantiation. Perhaps not un-expectedly, we can agree that the experts are often right; but not always.

Readers will also note that I am quoting the views of experts in pref-erence to the generalized conclusions of research into the effects of ad-vertisements (copytesting) in theaters and in homes and, indeed, any type of advertising research. My experience tells me that both the ex-perts and the research are fallible, but I believe the experts are much less so. They are also considerably more enjoyable to read.

Intrinsically Likable

Advertising is totally ineffective unless some people, at least, are pre-pared to look at it. This is one of the reasons that advertising communi-cation is such a difficult art. All viewers, listeners, and readers can recognize what advertising is, and most people turn away from it as an immediate and automatic reaction. The advertising writer's first task is therefore to think of a message compelling enough—or friendly and involving enough—to cause some consumers to pause before they switch off their mental engagement—and then to stimulate some of the people who pause to go on further.

There is no formula for doing this, but it is a striking feature of the Alpha One campaigns that the advertisers in every case managed to hold viewers' attention by giving a reward for watching. This is done by mak-ing the commercials engaging, entertaining, lighthearted, and amusing to look at. The advertisers address viewers as their equals and do not talk down to them. They respect the public's intelligence.

In some cases, the commercial is slightly incomplete, and the viewer is encouraged to take a modest step to understand what it is about. In other cases, the commercial springs a surprise—there is something un-expected that intrigues the person looking at it. A few of these success-ful commercials are both incomplete and unexpected (the qualities have a natural affinity).

The commercials are often amusing, but they tend not to employ broad humor. A striking characteristic of the sound tracks of the commercials is their generally understated tone of voice. This is often slightly ironic, as if the advertisers do not take themselves too seriously. This tone is appealing to viewers and persuades them to form a bond with the adver-tisers, based on the relevance of the brand and how it is presented. Mu-sic also has an important role in many commercials.

The ability of a commercial to entertain is occasionally at odds with how strongly it can sell (and vice versa). A commercial is nothing more than a piece of paid-for communication with a behavioral objective. With the most effective commercials, the entertainment is embedded in the brand. The entertainment in the commercial generates a warm glow that is directed toward the brand and, in the most successful campaigns, can actually surround it.

"You can't save souls in an empty church."—David Ogilvy[1]

"Boredom with life is so widespread a disease that I reckon the first big job we have to do in advertising is to be interesting."—James Webb Young[2]

"Our problem is they don't even hate us. They are just bored with us. And the surest way to produce boredom is to do what everybody else is doing."—William Bernbach[3]

"If the public is bored today—then let's blame it on the fact that it is being handed boring messages created by bored advertising people."—Leo Burnett[4]

"You should try to charm the consumer into buying your product."—David Ogilvy[5]

"Whether the ad made a friend or an enemy out of her before she listened to what it had to say . . . this thoroughly unreasonable and irrational initial reaction to an ad must be almost as important as what the ad actually had to say."—Leo Burnett[6]

"We try to make our advertising 'fun to look at'—exciting to look at—but never forced, and right on the subject of the product itself. We maintain that every product has inherent drama."—Leo Burnett[7]

"If advertising did not contain an element of reward, either in the form of information, entertainment, or some aesthetic compensation, we would be a mass of raving maniacs."—Leo Burnett[8]

"We still don't have research that really tells us a very simple thing—Do people like or dislike an ad?"—Leo Burnett[9]

"Yesterday's discoveries are today's commonplaces; a daringly fresh image soon becomes stale by repetition, degenerates into a cliché, and loses its emotive appeal."—Arthur Koestler[10]

"How do you storyboard a smile? Yet the quality of that smile may make the difference between a commercial that works and one that doesn't work."—William Bernbach[11]

"Music actually provides a measure of pleasurable entertainment. Some 'entertainment,' even when irrelevant to the product, may provide a modest benefit to an advertisement."—Alfred Politz[12]

"Advertising should be regarded as a branch of show business."—Randall Rothenberg[13]

"Agencies are indulging in a lot of campaigns which burnish their reputations for 'creativity' but do not try to sell the product."—David Ogilvy[14]

"Humor depends primarily on its surprise effect."—Arthur Koestler[15]

"All patterns of creative activity are trivalent: they can enter the service of humor, discovery, or art."—Arthur Koestler[16]

"Until 1976, Procter and Gamble eschewed music, but they are now using it, albeit in only 10 percent of their commercials. And they now use a touch of humor in some of their commercials."—David Ogilvy[17]

"Selling consumers through humor requires a very special talent. Today, within both agency and client organizations, too much caution prevails. There are too many grim and unhappy faces."—Amil Gargano[18]

"Advertising today serves up dramatic moments loaded with indirect sales appeals. By skillfully blending emotional and pragmatic appeals, and by camouflaging persuasion with wit and entertainment, advertisers allow consumers to draw their own conclusions about the brand and its advantages."—David N. Martin[19]

"Advertising still downgrades the consumer's intelligence because the people who are doing the ads are often as stupid as the people they think they're talking to."—Jerry Della Femina[20]

"Thou shalt honor the public's intelligence."—Leo Burnett[21]

"The consumer isn't a moron; she is your wife."—David Ogilvy[22]

Visual

The most powerful cultural trend during the past half-century has been the development of visual literacy—the growth in communication by images and symbols. This is true of all societies, from the most educated to the least, and it is of course a direct result of the growth of television. The accompanying decline in verbal literacy is an even more important—and totally deplorable—phenomenon, but this is not the place to discuss and lament it.

Television, the main engine driving the growth of visual communication, is also the main medium for packaged goods advertising. Advertisers would be acting against their self-interest if they did not exploit television's potential, in particular its power to demonstrate and its ability to generate mood and emotion. The Alpha One campaigns are models in this regard. And the views of our experts are, as usual, illuminating.

(From a speech delivered at a professional conference) "Everything we have done today has been in the language of words. And our market out there for most of the products that most all of us sell involves talking to people for whom words are really going out of style."—William M. Backer[23]

"I sometimes think that a good commercial should only have two words in the beginning that said simply, 'Watch this.'"—David Ogilvy[24]

"We can all point to many cases where the image is remembered long after the words are forgotten."—Leo Burnett[25]

"Demonstrations don't have to be dull. To demonstrate how strong paper-board can be, International Paper spanned a canyon with a bridge made of paper-board—and then drove a heavy truck over it."—David Ogilvy[26]

An advertisement "can project a unique selling proposition (USP) without using any words whatsoever. Johnson & Johnson ran a superb advertisement which showed an egg, stuck to a Band-Aid, immersed in a clear glass vessel of boiling water."—Rosser Reeves[27]

For food advertising "build your advertisement around appetite appeal. The larger your food illustration, the more appetite appeal."—David Ogilvy[28]

"I now know that in television you must make your pictures tell the story. Try running your commercial with the sound turned off; if it doesn't sell without sound, it is useless."—David Ogilvy[29]

"There is another gambit available which can move mountains: emotion and mood. Most commercials slide off [the viewer's] memory like water off a duck's back. For this reason you should give your commercials a touch of singularity, a burr that will make them stick in the viewer's mind. But be very careful how you do this; the viewer is apt to remember your burr but forget your selling promise."—David Ogilvy[30]

"A look or a take from an actor or actress can often register consumer satisfaction better than any words can."—Alvin Hampel[31]

"The ability to travel from place to place is the purpose served by an automobile. Is this a sales point? No, it is not. Safety provided by an automobile is not its main purpose. Is it nevertheless a sales point? No, it is not. The look of an automobile is not its main purpose, but it is a sales point."—Alfred Politz[32]

Communicating Their Promise in Terms Relevant to Consumers

Consumers buy brands for the benefits that those brands give them. But a manufacturer should not expect success in a highly competitive world if an ad communicates merely a bald functional advantage, even if that brand is the only one to offer it. Functional benefits are very important, but advertising claims about them are processed in two ways in the consumer's psyche.

First, a functional advantage is often broadened in the consumer's mind into something much more emotional. This has a stronger effect than functional claims on their own, and the resulting amalgam is unique to the brand. The manufacturer's prospects are improved to the extent that this happens. A statement in an advertisement for a food brand that it contains no cholesterol or sugar or salt releases a torrent of emotional signals about health and long life. The click of a camera shutter in a commercial can be transformed in the viewer's mind into a highly charged message: this click records—and in effect freezes—the high points in the consumer's life.

The second way in which claims are processed is that the functional (or the functional-cum-emotional) qualities of a brand are perceived as having value to the consumer solely to the extent that they relate to her day-to-day life. Unless a brand has functional features superior to the competition in at least some respects, it will not be bought repeatedly. But these alone are not enough. The consumer must find the brand's functional features more relevant than the advantages offered by any competitive brands she may be considering at the time.

It follows that unless the consumer is shown a brand's qualities in highly personal and relevant terms, it will have no appeal. Advertisers therefore study their buyers. The positioning of their brands (determining where their brands fit into a competitive market place) and the creative idea, are both the direct result of the advertisers' knowledge of their consumers.

One rather obvious point is that advertising that depicts people is likely to be more successful than advertising that does not. Qualitative research has shown that advertising about products on their own can generate cold, impersonal image associations.

The positioning of the brand in relation to its competitors must be thought out with agonizing precision. This positioning embraces both the brand's functional and its nonfunctional features. When CD—an important brand of which I have firsthand knowledge—was first introduced, its selected positioning was the end product of an extraordinary process of experimentation that involved writing and testing nineteen alternative positions in the form of more or less finished films. The cost of this film production was many millions of dollars, and perhaps more seriously, the procedure took more than two years. But the result repaid the cost and trouble, because the brand was and is a triumph in the market place. It is no coincidence that it has one of the highest STAS differentials measured by Nielsen.

An even more important point about functional features is that advertising that sells them successfully must be based on an idea. As I have already implied, this idea can be—and generally is—enclosed in an emotional envelope. But if the idea is going to work at all, this envelope must contain something important to the consumer. The commercials should be likable—but the selling message must be unmistakable.

In successful campaigns, the rational features of the brand are almost invariably demonstrated. The purpose of this strategy is partly to provide a rational selling argument and partly to provide the consumer with a postpurchase rationalization: a justification for a preference that may have been totally nonrational. Psychologists have a name for this curious effect; they call it the reduction of cognitive dissonance.

"After studying just why [a magazine publisher] is so successful we have come to the conclusion that it all rests on just one thing: He doesn't sell space; he sells ideas."—James Webb Young[33]

"I doubt if more than one campaign in a hundred contains a big idea. I am supposed to be one of the more fertile inventors of big ideas, but in my long career as a copywriter I have not had more than twenty, if that." —David Ogilvy[34]

"The advertisement may have said five, ten, or fifteen things, but the consumer will tend to pick out just one, or else, in a fumbling, confused way, he tries to fuse them together into a concept of his own."—Rosser Reeves[35]

"Ads are planned and written with some utterly wrong conception. They are written to please the seller. The interests of the buyer are forgotten."— Claude C. Hopkins[36]

"You can attain a temporary share of market with a new product or a smart promotion, but to enjoy a really healthy share of market (in three years) you have to start now, to build a share of mind."—Leo Burnett[37]

"I agree with Roy Whittier who once said, 'Too many advertisements spend so much time telling why the product is best that they fail to tell why it's good.'"—Leo Burnett[38]

"If a product has features worth paying money for, it must have features worth paying attention to."—Alfred Politz[39]

"We start with people."—Alfred Politz[40]

"Reasoning and emotion are not opposite to one another, any more than temperature and size in the physical world are opposites. Both reasoning and emotion are genuine reactions. They are distinctly different, and yet they influence each other."—Alfred Politz[41]

"The key is to find out which button you can press on every person that makes him want to buy your product over another product. What's the emotional thing that affects people?"—Jerry Della Femina[42]

"Researchers have not yet found a way to quantify the effectiveness of emotion, but I have come to believe that commercials with a large content of nostalgia, charm, and even sentimentality can be enormously effective. . . . I hasten to add that consumers also need a rational excuse to justify their emotional decisions."—David Ogilvy[43]

"I am astonished to find how many manufacturers, on both sides of the Atlantic, still believe that women can be persuaded by logic and argument to buy one brand in preference to another. The greater the similarity between products, the less part reason plays in brand selection."—David Ogilvy[44]

"A better way may be found through the use of advertising to add a subjective value to the tangible values of the product. For subjective values are no less real than the tangible ones."—James Webb Young[45]

"Most people and propositions have their natural limitations. These are inherent in personality and temperament if in nothing else. Advertising which keys a proposition to a certain kind of person may be highly successful as long as it stays true to type. When it tries to be all things to all men it endangers the personality it has established and makes an appeal to nobody."—James Webb Young[46]

"Promise, large promise is the soul of an advertisement."—Samuel Johnson[47]

A letter from David Ogilvy forms a fitting conclusion to this chapter (see page 80). He sent me this letter shortly after the first edition of this book came out. As readers can see, this chapter made sense to him although he was frankly perplexed by the rest of the book. I was subsequently relieved to know that a number of other prominent advertising people in many countries around the world were less puzzled by what I had written!

Notes

1. David Ogilvy, *Confessions of an Advertising Man* (New York: Atheneum, 1963; repr. 1984) p. 97.
2. James Webb Young, *The Diary of an Ad Man* (Lincolnwood, Chicago: NTC Business Books, 1990), p. 227.
3. William Bernbach, *Creativity in Advertising: What It Is, and Isn't* (New York: Association of National Advertisers, 1965), pp. 1–2.
4. Leo Burnett, *Communications of an Advertising Man* (Chicago: privately published, 1961), p. 25.
5. Ogilvy, *Confessions of an Advertising Man*, p. 98.
6. Burnett, *Communications of an Advertising Man*, p. 65.
7. Ibid., p. 272.

8. Ibid., p. 47.

9. Ibid., p. 64.

10. Arthur Koestler, *The Act of Creation* (New York: Macmillan, 1969), p. 335.

11. William Bernbach, *Beware of Arithmetic* (New York: Association of National Advertisers, 1973), pp. 5–6.

12. Alfred Politz, *The Politz Papers: Science and Truth in Marketing Research,* ed. Hugh S. Hardy (Chicago: American Marketing Association, 1990), p. 170.

13. Randall Rothenberg, personal communication, 1993.

14. David Ogilvy, personal communication, October 4, 1993.

15. Koestler, *Act of Creation*, p. 91.

16. Ibid., p. 27.

17. David Ogilvy, *Ogilvy on Advertising* (New York: Crown, 1983), p. 157.

18. Amil Gargano, *Thoughts on Comparative and Humorous Advertising* (New York: Association of National Advertisers, 1984), p. 8.

19. David N. Martin, *Romancing the Brand* (New York: American Management Association, 1989), p. 139.

20. Jerry Della Femina, *From Those Wonderful Folks Who Gave You Pearl Harbor* (London: Pan Books, 1970), p. 26.

21. Burnett, *Communications of an Advertising Man,* p. 95.

22. Ogilvy, *Confessions of an Advertising Man*, p. 96.

23. William M. Backer, *What the Creative Wants from the Researcher* (New York: Association of National Advertisers, 1983), p. 4.

24. David Ogilvy, *The Art of Writing Advertising,* ed. Dennis Higgins (Chicago: Advertising Publications, 1965), p. 90.

25. Burnett, *Communications of an Advertising Man*, p. 37.

26. Ogilvy, *Ogilvy on Advertising*, p. 107.

27. Rosser Reeves, *Reality in Advertising* (New York: Alfred A Knopf, 1961), p. 69.

28. Ogilvy, *Confessions of an Advertising Man*, p. 135.

29. Ibid., p. 130.

30. Ibid., p. 132.

31. Alvin Hampel, *It's Never Been Done Before . . . and Other Obstacles to Creativity* (New York: Association of National Advertisers, 1977), p. 4.

32. Politz, *The Politz Papers*, p. 142.

33. James Webb Young, *A Technique for Producing Ideas* (Chicago: Crain Communications, 1940, repr. 1972), p. 10.

34. Ogilvy, *Ogilvy on Advertising*, p. 16.

35. Reeves, *Reality in Advertising*, p. 34.

36. Claude C. Hopkins, *Scientific Advertising* (Chicago: Crain Books, 1966), p. 225.

37. Burnett, *Communications of an Advertising Man*, p. 82.

38. Ibid., p. 187.

39. Politz, *The Politz Papers*, p. 43.

40. Ibid., p. 130.

41. Ibid., pp. 147–148.

42. Della Femina, *From Those Wonderful Folks*, p. 126.

43. Ogilvy, *Ogilvy on Advertising*, p. 109.

44. David Ogilvy, *The Unpublished David Ogilvy* (New York: Ogilvy Group, 1986), pp. 77–78.

45. James Webb Young, *How to Become an Advertising Man* (Chicago: Crain Books, 1979), p. 73.

46. Young, *Diary of an Ad Man*, pp. 181–182.

47. Dr. Samuel Johnson, *The Idler*, No. 41.

Figure 6.1   **A Letter From David Ogilvy to the Author**

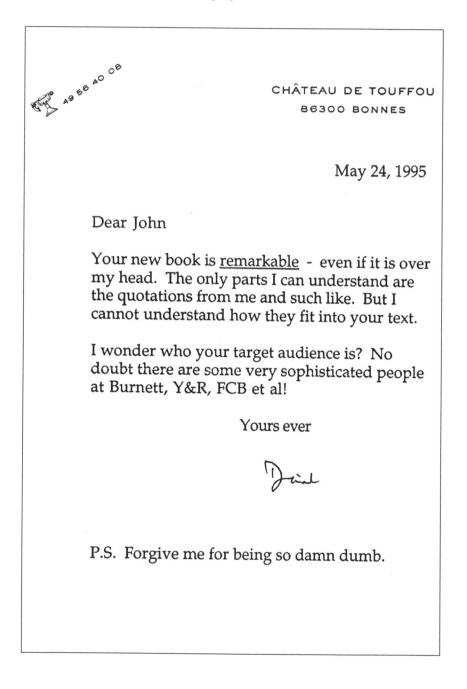

CHÂTEAU DE TOUFFOU
86300 BONNES

May 24, 1995

Dear John

Your new book is <u>remarkable</u> - even if it is over
my head. The only parts I can understand are
the quotations from me and such like. But I
cannot understand how they fit into your text.

I wonder who your target audience is? No
doubt there are some very sophisticated people
at Burnett, Y&R, FCB et al!

Yours ever

II

Evidence for Part I
Seventy-eight Brands Dissected

7

Advertising That Works
The Alpha One Brands

Chapters 7, 8, 9, and 10 should be read as a coordinated sequence. Each is devoted to one of the groups of brands described toward the end of Chapter 2. The purpose of analyzing these groups is that they provide the supporting evidence on which the conclusions in Part 1 are based.

To help the reader, I shall repeat two definitions used in Part I. Medium-term sales growth (or decline) is based on Nielsen data measuring a brand's market share in the first quarter of 1991, indexed as 100. The average share for the second, third, and fourth quarters has an index number calculated to compare it with the first quarter's figure. The short-term advertising strength (STAS) differential index is the stimulated STAS for each brand, indexed on its baseline STAS, which is measured as 100.

Three important variables, all controlled by the marketer, have a direct influence on sales. They are a brand's advertising intensity, price index, and promotional intensity.

Advertising intensity is represented by the brand's share of total advertising in its category (i.e., share of voice), divided by its share of market. This produces an estimate of the percentage points of advertising voice for each percentage point of a brand's market share. In this way, we can compare brands of different sizes according to their relative investment in advertising. The calculation is explained in more detail in Appendix D; the measure of share of voice is based on Nielsen data.

Although Chapter 5 demonstrates that a brand's advertising budget has

Table 7.1

Medium-Term Share Growth/Decline Index in Each Quintile in Four Independent Quintile Analyses

	STAS differential	Advertising intensity	Price index	Promotional intensity
Total	106	106	106	106
Top quintile	132	132	101	120
Second quintile	99	100	99	109
Third quintile	100	97	95	101
Fourth quintile	99	103	104	98
Bottom quintile	100	99	133	102

little influence within the purchase interval so long as most consumers are exposed to at least one advertisement for the brand, it is a different matter when we are looking at more extended periods. Over a year, the continuity of a schedule is important, because continuous advertising reduces the number of sales down over the twelve months. Continuity is a question of the advertising budget, measured here as advertising intensity.

The price index is a measure of the average price paid by consumers for the brand, compared with the average price in the category (indexed as 100).

Promotional intensity is measured by the percentage of the brand's volume sold on deal (i.e., at a special, reduced price), compared with the category average (indexed as 100). A brand's promotional intensity is related to its price index, but the two are not the same. The price index is the brand's list price less all the promotional allowances made to the consumer. The total amount of such allowances is measured by the index of promotional intensity, and this index signals the importance of the brand's short-term price reductions as a tactical selling tool.

Note that the price index and promotional intensity are expressions of consumer promotions, intended to pull the merchandise through the retail pipeline. The analysis does not cover trade promotions, which are mainly financial incentives to the retail trade aimed at pushing the goods through the pipeline to the consumer. Even though this activity is not measured in my calculations, I do not imply that trade promotions have no influence on consumer sales. Trade promotions are often partially passed on to the consumer in the form of retail price reductions, which are of course covered in this analysis. (A common example is when stores double the value of manufacturers' coupons.)

Table 7.1 is based on a quintile analysis. Brands are ranked in five separate groups from highest to lowest according to a specific measure.

Table 7.2

Composition of the Four Groups of Brands

	Number	Percent
Total	78	100
Alpha One	26	33
Alpha Two	19	24
Beta	20	26
Gamma	13	17

The table in fact describes four such measures: STAS differential, advertising intensity, price, and promotional intensity. For each quintile for each of the four measures, I have worked out the *medium-term growth in sales* and presented it in indexed form. This is an attempt to tease out what inputs—STAS, advertising intensity, price, and promotional intensity—actually contribute most to increasing sales.

There is only one clear finding from Table 7.1. The top quintiles of STAS differential, advertising intensity, and promotional intensity are associated with high sales increases, and there is the expected relationship between price and sales, with the highest price associated with low sales growth. Beyond this, the picture is too complex to provide meaningful answers. We must therefore subdivide the brands in a different way, as is done in Table 7.2.

The number of brands in each of the four groups discussed in Chapters 7, 8, 9, and 10 respectively is shown in Table 7.2. I have followed the normal statistical convention of putting the percentages in parentheses to warn readers that they are calculated from a total of only seventy-eight brands. The percentages represent a statistical projection, which would not be the case if the total were 100 or more.

From now on, each group of brands will be treated separately, starting with Alpha One. These are the majority of the brands with both a positive STAS differential and medium-term share growth over the course of one year. A small number of large brands, those in the Beta group, also had these characteristics.

The Alpha One Brands Described

Table 7.3 shows the composition of the Alpha One group. The starting point for this analysis was two measures of market place success, STAS and medium-term share growth, and the brands are ranked by the latter.

Table 7.3

Alpha One Brands

Brand	Market share first-quarter 1991 (percent)	Medium-term share growth (index)	STAS differential (index)	Advertising intensity (percent)	Price (index)	Promotional intensity (index)
LF	2.7	100	120	2.6	110	91
JC	8.2	100	167	0.9	101	146
LCC	2.7	103	157	2.6	130	108
DD	8.0	105	108	2.0	157	94
AK	3.4	106	181	1.2	66	116
LC	4.0	107	100	2.0	91	107
LJ	1.5	107	100	3.3	88	131
AE	5.4	107	119	2.2	105	118
BD	6.2	108	153	0.5	95	139
CH	4.2	109	121	2.4	143	94
DH	2.9	110	156	2.8	75	121
LD	3.2	112	111	2.5	84	119
MG	2.1	114	147	7.1	130	85
AL	2.9	114	160	3.4	73	128
BP	3.8	118	149	1.9	90	64
KD	3.1	119	106	5.2	87	100
EE	6.1	120	204	1.0	94	115
KG	1.9	121	142	2.7	113	83
LG	2.3	122	121	2.2	127	70
LCCC	1.3	123	119	4.6	123	123
BR	2.0	125	133	5.0	109	108
KH	1.5	127	106	0.4	75	90
AJ	2.4	158	232	1.2	81	123
CD	5.0	178	193	2.0	82	122
AH	2.6	219	253	3.5	97	163
CN	1.0	330	151	9.0	46	159
Average	3.5	129	147	2.9	99	112

Medium-term share growth is not itself a marketing input, but an outcome. However, from a comparison of this and the four marketing stimuli, we should be able to infer what has caused the share growth if we look at the variables closely enough.

The most obvious features of Table 7.3 are that the STAS differential varies but is quite pronounced in most cases; advertising investments are skewed, with only eight brands spending more than the average ratio; and price is a more general marketing stimulus, with fifteen brands being priced below the mean. A related point is the general prevalence of promotions, with fourteen brands having above-average promotional ratios. The data in the table also contain some more subtle points.

The medium-term share growth index is described technically as a dependent variable. The four marketing stimuli are independent variables, and I am concerned with the influence of each of these on the dependent one. (As explained earlier, the price index and promotional intensity index are not independent of each other, although the degree of dependence of share growth on either or both of them is something we can look at.)

If we run down each column of figures in Table 7.3, there seems to be no close relationship between any one of the independent variables and the dependent one. But connecting relationships exist, and to uncover them we have to do some averaging. Note that when we relate the four marketing variables to the outcome, the share growth index, we are looking at the combined effect of short- and long-term stimuli. (I later show a way of separating these effects.)

In looking at the relative importance of the four stimuli, I have analyzed the data in three ways, with the following objectives: to establish how different intensities of each of the four marketing inputs influence share growth, to measure any synergy between the various marketing stimuli, and to isolate the stimuli that best explain the varying amounts of share growth for different brands.

Different Intensities of the Four Marketing Stimuli

A total of twenty-six brands is too small to break into quintiles. However, I am comfortable about dividing the total into two groups for each of the marketing inputs: the brands that receive above-average and those that receive below-average amounts of each stimulus. The results, measured by share growth, are seen in Table 7.4.

Two things can be inferred from Table 7.4. First, as already noted, advertisers made a greater commitment to price-oriented activities than to advertising activities: there are fifteen brands driven by low price and fourteen by high promotions, compared with thirteen brands with a strong STAS differential and only eight with a high advertising investment. These brand numbers are not an accident, but represent management choices. Except in the cases of high STAS, the brands driven by the other marketing inputs represent decisions on the part of manufacturing companies: decisions that tend to favor price stimuli more strongly than advertising stimuli.

Table 7.4

Alpha One Brands: Medium-Term Share Growth From Different Amounts of Marketing Stimuli

	Total		Above-average input		Below-average input	
	Number of brands	Average medium -term share growth index	Number of brands	Average medium -term share growth index	Number of brands	Average medium -term share growth index
STAS differential	26	129	13	144	13	114
Advertising intensity	26	129	8	155	18	117
Price	26	129	11	112	15	142
Promotional intensity	26	129	14	142	12	114

The second inference from the table is that although above-average amounts of all the stimuli work well, the advertising-related activities work just as strongly as—and perhaps more strongly than—the price-related activities. Some readers may find this surprising in view of the general rule that promotions generate more immediate sales than advertising. However, Table 7.4 is analyzing a medium-term sales response, not a short-term one.

Readers will remember from the quintile analysis earlier in this chapter the overlap between the four marketing stimuli. Virtually all the Alpha One brands are driven by two stimuli, and a few are driven by three. The combined effect of these on share growth is seen in Table 7.5. In this table, promotional intensity has been omitted because of its overlap with price.

This table isolates the brands that received above-average amounts of the two remaining marketing stimuli—advertising intensity and price reduction—on top of a positive STAS effect. Advertising intensity was measured by whether the brand's intensity is above the average for all brands of the same market share (based on Table 12.1 in Chapter 12). Brands with a price index of less than 100 were selected because their prices are below their category averages (therefore offering a greater-than-average price incentive).

Despite the small subsamples on which Table 7.5 is based, four conclusions emerge.

1. For the Alpha One brands, the STAS effect alone (with below-average amounts of the other sales stimuli) produces a lift of 32 percent in share within the seven-day period and 11 percent over the course of the year.

Table 7.5

**Alpha One Brands: Share Growth From Different Combinations of
Marketing Stimuli**

	Number of brands	Average STAS differential	Average medium-term share growth index
Baseline		100	100
STAS differential alone	7	132	111
STAS differential and advertising intensity	5	126	112
STAS differential and price	7	162	121
STAS differential and advertising intensity and price	7	160	168

2. The addition of above-average advertising intensity adds nothing to the STAS effect.

3. Adding the above-average price stimulus to the STAS effect *doubles the short-term effect.* This can be explained by advertising that triggers consumers to buy promoted merchandise. The medium-term effect is also doubled from the level stimulated by STAS alone.

4. Adding the above-average price stimulus and above-average advertising intensity to the effect of the STAS differential causes no further short-term lift beyond that stimulated by price, but it causes a powerful synergy in the long term. The increase in share over a year is *six times higher that the STAS effect alone.* This increase underscores the value of integrated planning of all marketing activities. This is an extremely important point.

The Stimuli That Best Explain Share Growth

The best way to isolate the stimuli that most closely explain share growth is to start with the dependent variable—medium-term share growth itself—and to group the twenty-six brands according to the amounts by which they increased. We can then compare these families of brands with the sales stimuli (the amounts of which vary for each group of brands). The sample is not large enough to employ a quintile analysis. But I can use terciles, an analysis that isolates three groups of brands: the nine brands with the lowest share growth, the nine brands with the highest share growth, and the eight brands in between.

The important point about this analysis is that it can detect the varying

Table 7.6

Alpha One Brands: In Terciles

Tercile	Medium-term share growth (index)	STAS differential (index)	Advertising intensity (percent)	Price (index)	Promotional intensity (index)
Top nine brands	167	161	3.4	95	116
Middle eight brands	115	144	3.3	97	103
Bottom nine brands	105	134	1.9	105	117
All brands	129	147	2.9	99	112

Table 7.7

Alpha One Brands: Tercile Index

Tercile	Medium-term share growth	STAS differential	Advertising intensity	Price	Promotional intensity
Top nine brands	159	120	179	90	99
Middle eight brands	110	107	174	92	88
Bottom nine brands	100	100	100	100	100

quantities of the different marketing inputs that have influenced the market place success of the separate groups of brands—that is, it can indicate what degree of advertising intensity is associated with the least successful brands and what degree is associated with the most successful ones. Table 7.6 shows the results, and Table 7.7 indexes the same figures.

Comparing the tercile analysis of share growth with those for the four marketing stimuli, we see some sort of relationship for the STAS differential, advertising intensity, and price (remembering that the price relationship is reciprocal). There is, however, no relationship at all with promotional intensity. And the only measure that indicates the rather large scope of the share growth is advertising intensity (advertising intensity growth of 79 percent in the top tercile; share growth of 59 percent). The STAS differential and price measures show much smaller numbers.

We have already seen (in Table 7.4) that both the advertising-related inputs produce medium-term share growth at least as large as—and perhaps larger than—the price-related stimuli. We now also see that advertising intensity is more correlated with share growth than are any of the other measures. This means that *advertising intensity more directly predicts share growth than any of the other variables.*

The lack of correlation between promotional intensity and share growth is evidence of the weak medium-term effect of promotions. Promotions have a powerful short-term influence on the sales of most brands, but this effect does not hold over the course of a year because of the effects of promotions for competitive brands. On the other hand, the short-term effect of advertising is more likely to lead to a medium-term effect, by the process described in Chapter 5.

STAS and Market Share

One of the most puzzling features of the research published in this book is the disparity between a brand's STAS and its market share. They both measure essentially the same thing, and the only difference is that STAS is a strictly short-term measure—share of purchases within the purchase interval—whereas market share covers a much longer period. Table 7.8 shows the STAS and share figures for the Alpha One brands. The achieved market share represents the average for the second, third, and fourth quarters of 1991.

Note that we are now looking at a trio of market share measures (and in this book the word *trio* will be used to describe them): the baseline STAS, representing the average, unstimulated share level; the stimulated STAS, representing the short-term effect of the campaign idea; and the achieved market share, representing the combined effect of the short-term STAS stimulus and the three other marketing stimuli, minus the countervailing influence of competitors' marketing activities. This combined effect represents a medium-term outcome.

Aggregate Effect of Short-Term and Medium-Term Stimuli

Table 7.8 has five noteworthy features.

1. The brands all have a positive STAS differential (this is of course a characteristic of all Alpha brands).
2. In most cases the difference between the baseline STAS and the achieved market share is relatively small. On average, the achieved market share is 5 percent higher.

Table 7.8

Alpha One Brands: Trio of Market Share Measure

Brand	Baseline STAS	Stimulated STAS	Achieved market share
LF	2.5	3.0	2.7
JC	7.0	11.7	8.2[a]
LCC	3.0	4.7	2.8
DD	7.8	8.4	8.4
AK	2.6	4.7	3.6[a]
LC	7.1	7.1	4.3
LJ	2.1	2.1	1.6
AE	8.3	9.9	5.8
BD	6.2	9.5	6.7
CH	3.3	4.0	4.6[a]
DH	3.4	5.3	3.2
LD	4.7	5.2	3.6
MG	1.5	2.2	2.4[a]
AL	3.0	4.8	3.3[a]
BP	3.3	4.9	4.5[a]
KD	3.1	3.6	3.7[a]
EE	5.2	10.6	7.3[a]
KG	1.2	1.7	2.3[a]
LG	2.4	2.9	2.8[a]
LCCC	1.6	1.9	1.6
BR	2.4	3.2	2.5
KH	3.3	3.5	1.9
AJ	3.7	8.6	3.8
CD	7.2	13.9	8.9[a]
AH	4.9	12.4	5.7[a]
CN	3.9	5.9	3.3
All brands	4.0	6.0	4.2

[a]Brands with a minimum of 10 percent lift from baseline STAS to achieved market share.

3. The relatively small average difference between baseline STAS and achieved market share is less important than the fact that the achieved market share always represents an improvement in the second, third, and fourth quarters over the first-quarter level. This improvement demonstrates the effectiveness of the various marketing stimuli.

4. The fourth point relates to the most powerful brands in the short plus medium term. All the brands in the Alpha One group are successful in the sense that their advertising campaigns are creatively effective. In addition, there is some upward progress in

their market share over the course of the year. However, judged by the rigorous criterion of the extent by which the achieved market share exceeds the baseline STAS, the average lift is, as already mentioned, only 5 percent. But some brands achieve a minimum lift of 10 percent. These are indicated in Table 7.8.

5. Two-thirds of the brands in this very successful group achieve a lift of at least 20 percent between baseline STAS and achieved market share. About half this increase is a result of synergy between the various marketing inputs.

Separating the Medium-Term From the Short-Term Effects

Since the increase (if any) from a brand's baseline STAS to its stimulated STAS isolates the short-term creative effect of its advertising campaign, it follows logically that any change from the stimulated STAS to the achieved market share captures the medium-term effect of the campaign, against the efforts of competitive brands. This competitive activity inhibits most brands, so that, although the STAS differential is positive (for the Alpha One group), there is a drop between the stimulated STAS and the achieved market share.

In their drop from stimulated STAS to achieved market share, some brands hold up better than others. The twelve most successful ones are analyzed in Table 7.9. (In this book these will be referred to as the top performance brands.) The fourteen least successful appear in Table 7.10. These tables are a real measure of the effectiveness of those parts of the marketing mix other than the creative content of the campaign.

Two important points emerge from Table 7.9 and Table 7.10.

First, as might be expected, the top performance brands have on average relatively higher advertising investments. The difference between an average advertising intensity of 3.4 percent and one of 2.5 percent is large and would in most cases represent considerable dollar amounts. This means that the schedules of the more successful brands have the funds to provide greater continuity, thus helping to maintain these brands' ups against the advertising and promotional activities of competitors.

The second feature relates to price. The average price of the top performance brands is 22 percent more than that of the less successful ones (20 percentaged on 92). This indicates that buyers value the successful brands more than do the buyers of the less successful brands. This sup-

Table 7.9

**Brands That Most Successfully Maintain Their Stimulated STAS:
The Top Performance Alpha One Brands**

Brand	Percent change from stimulated STAS to achieved market share	Advertising intensity (percent)	Price (index)
LF	−10	2.6	110
DD	no change	2.0	157
AK	−23	1.2	66
LJ	−24	3.3	88
CH	+15	2.4	143
MG	+9	7.1	130
BP	−8	1.9	90
KD	+3	5.2	87
KG	+35	2.7	113
LG	−3	2.2	127
LCCC	−16	4.6	123
BR	−22	5.0	109
Average	−4	3.4	112

Table 7.10

**Alpha One Brands That Are Least Successful in Maintaining Their
Stimulated STAS**

Brand	Percent change from stimulated STAS to achieved market share	Advertising intensity (percent)	Price (index)
JC	−30	0.9	101
LCC	−40	2.6	130
LC	−39	2.0	91
AE	−41	2.0	157
BD	−30	0.5	95
DH	−40	2.8	75
LD	−31	3.3	88
AL	−31	3.4	73
EE	−31	1.0	94
KH	−46	0.4	75
AJ	−56	1.2	81
CD	−36	2.0	82
AH	−54	3.5	97
CN	−46	9.0	46
Average	−39	2.5	92

ports the theory that advertising generates a long-term effect. Successful advertising builds added values. It works in cooperation with repeat purchase. And the value of the brand is gradually but significantly augmented in the minds of its users. They will pay more money for it.

Twelve Things We Have Learned About the Alpha One Brands

1. In an initial topline analysis, the three main marketing stimuli—the creative content, the advertising budget, and the promotions—affect the seventy-eight advertised brands in this research in a similar way.
2. The Alpha One group comprises twenty-six brands with a combination of positive STAS and medium-term market share growth. Within this group, there is much variability among the STAS differentials and the share improvements, but in many cases both are pronounced.
3. More manufacturers follow a price/promotional strategy than follow an advertising-driven strategy, although there is some overlap between the two.
4. When we examine the aggregate effect of all marketing stimuli, the medium-term outcome of the price/promotional strategy is weaker than that of the advertising-driven strategy. (Promotions are almost always more effective in the short term, when measured in sales. They are, however, generally unprofitable.)
5. The brands that are driven by a double strategy of advertising plus promotions generate a powerful synergy.
6. The only marketing input that is reasonably correlated with (and therefore probably predictive of) market share growth is advertising intensity—advertising pressure and market share follow each other in a crude but unmistakable fashion. This confirms a number of other studies that demonstrate the same phenomenon. But remember that the Alpha One brands all have a positive STAS differential.
7. When we compare the trio of market share measures, the normal pattern (for the Alpha One brands at least) is a rise from the baseline STAS to the stimulated STAS, followed by a fall to the achieved market share, which represents the brand's response to pressure from competitive brands.

8. After discounting the short-term rise and fall, the net rise from baseline STAS to achieved market share is on average only 5 percent. But for twelve of the twenty-six brands, it is larger. This is a reflection of the above-average success of those brands' marketing mix in a competitive market place.

9. Of the twelve most successful brands, two-thirds show a lift of at least 20 percent from baseline STAS to achieved market share. I believe that a substantial amount of this increase is caused by synergy between the different marketing stimuli.

10. There is almost always a decline from the level of the stimulated STAS to the achieved market share, caused by the activities of competitive brands. But some brands fall less than others, as a consequence of the greater *long-term productivity* of their marketing stimuli.

11. As can been seen in Tables 7.9 and 7.10, the top performance brands (i.e., those that show the smallest drop from stimulated STAS to achieved market share) are significantly more advertising-driven than the less successful ones. There is an even more remarkable correlation. The top performance brands—those driven by advertising investment—are able to support a *much higher price* than the less successful brands.

12. In this analysis, therefore, when we look at the overall progress of all the brands, advertising plays a marginally more decisive role in achieving sales successes than do the other sales stimuli, although there is strong synergy between all the marketing inputs when they are applied together. However, when we isolate the specific medium-term factors (as opposed to the short-term ones) and when we in turn isolate the top performance brands, these are advertising-driven to a decisive degree. And the resultant improvement in value perceptions on the part of the consumers leads to these brands commanding significantly higher prices than the less successful brands can. The apparent inner strength and drive—the internal momentum—of these brands means that they do not require heavy and unprofitable promotions to boost their sales. The brands in this very special top-performance group total twelve out of our overall sample of seventy-eight.

The points listed above all hold important operational lessons for advertisers, detailed in Chapter 12.

8

Advertising That Stops Working
The Alpha Two Brands

The defining feature of the Alpha Two brands is that they combine a positive short-term advertising strength (STAS) differential (i.e., short-term share improvement) with no improvement in medium-term market share. There is undeniable evidence that their advertising campaigns yield results within seven days. But something intervenes to prevent this positive effect from being carried forward over the course of a year. Hence the title of this chapter.

The best way to describe this dissonance between short-term effectiveness and longer-term lack of effectiveness is to examine the averages of the Alpha Two brands' trio of market share measures, together with the average index of market share growth. These figures can then be compared with those for the Alpha One brands.

Table 8.1 shows that the STAS differential index is weaker for the Alpha Two brands than for Alpha One. But the major difference between the two groups is the negative trend in market share for Alpha Two, compared with the strongly positive trend for Alpha One. Remember that the market share growth shows each brand's development over the course of the year and is independent of the STAS differential, although the latter is one factor that influences it. With the Alpha One brands, the STAS effect works in conjunction with the other marketing stimuli to push sales upward. But the Alpha Two brands, despite their

Table 8.1

Alpha One and Alpha Two: Trio of Market Share Measures

	Average baseline STAS	Average stimulated STAS	Average achieved market share	Average index of medium-term growth/ decline
Alpha One	4.0 (= 100)	6.0 (= 150)	4.2 (= 105)	129
Alpha Two	4.5 (= 100)	5.9 (= 131)	4.1 (= 91)	83

positive STAS, are clearly inhibited by failures in some parts of their marketing inputs, which depress growth.

Table 8.2 summarizes the main details of the nineteen brands that make up the Alpha Two group. They are ranked according to the steepness of their share decline, starting with the most depressed brand.

If we compare the Alpha One brands (Table 7.3 in Chapter 7) with Alpha Two (Table 8.2) we see that:

- There are more Alpha One brands (twenty-six compared with nineteen).
- The average Alpha One brand grew by 29 percent; the average Alpha Two brand fell by 17 percent.
- The average STAS differential of the Alpha One brands is greater than that of the Alpha Two brands.[1]
- The average promotional intensity of the two groups is almost identical.
- The average advertising intensity of the Alpha One brands is 32 percent ahead of Alpha Two (and only seven of the latter brands are above the Alpha Two average).
- The average price of the Alpha Two brands is 19 percent above their category average (the comparable figure for Alpha One is 1 percent below). Since there is no difference in the promotional ratios of the two groups of brands, the higher prices of Alpha Two are a reflection of higher average list prices.

We can hypothesize that the weak sales performance of the Alpha Two brands is a result of their *relatively low advertising volume allied to their high list price* (despite the prevalence of reductions below the

Table 8.2

Alpha Two Brands

Brand	Market share first-quarter 1991 (percent)	Medium-term share decline (index)	STAS differential (index)	Advertising intensity (percent)	Price (index)	Promotional intensity (index)
BHH	7.3	42	121	1.6	116	88
LK	2.1	67	225	2.4	118	85
LE	4.3	74	121	2.1	110	106
CF	7.1	75	102	1.5	130	98
DE	6.4	75	111	2.3	155	81
AF	5.7	75	120	0.7	170	99
MF	2.9	76	102	1.7	91	188
LL	1.7	82	245	2.9	128	113
DF	4.7	83	118	2.8	92	116
AD	9.3	88	111	0.5	92	128
CJ	3.8	89	108	2.1	105	123
CE	8.2	90	124	1.7	144	93
JG	3.2	91	300	1.9	124	115
CG	5.6	95	102	0.7	137	98
MK	2.0	95	105	6.5	100	160
MB	7.8	96	114	2.4	135	126
AM	2.8	96	141	4.3	114	157
JF	3.2	97	187	1.6	81	96
LB	5.4	98	142	1.5	122	82
Average	4.9	83	142	2.2	119	113

rather high average). Taken together, these two factors are strong enough to negate the positive STAS differential of the Alpha Two brands.

So much for the bare essentials. But in the same way as I treated the Alpha One brands, we can get additional insights by doing some averaging.

In the analyses of the Alpha One brands, I looked first at the different amounts of the various marketing stimuli, to find out whether above-average quantities of these inputs generated above-average share growth (Table 7.5). This examination led in turn to a number of conclusions. Among these was the discovery of strong synergy between the different marketing inputs (Table 7.6).

Unfortunately, the data for the Alpha Two brands do not yield differences as important as those discovered for Alpha One. However, the third analysis I made of the Alpha One brands rang a bell when it was applied to Alpha Two.

Table 8.3

Alpha Two: Top Nine and Bottom Ten Brands

Subgroup	Medium-term share decline (index)	STAS differential (index)	Advertising intensity (percent)	Price (index)	Advertising intensity (index)
Top nine brands	94	147	2.5	118	117
Bottom ten brands	74	138	1.9	120	110

The Stimuli That Best Explain Different Rates of Decline

In the third analysis of the Alpha One brands, I isolated each brand's share growth as the dependent variable and clustered the Alpha One brands into subgroups based on this. I then worked out the average intensities or quantities of the different marketing inputs for the brands in each subgroup (Tables 7.7 and 7.8).

In similar fashion, I have divided the Alpha Two brands, breaking them down into two subgroups representing the brands that declined most (bottom ten brands) and those that declined least (top nine brands). I then calculated the average intensity or quantity of each marketing stimulus for each group (Table 8.3). The variations in the advertising-related measures are particularly evident. This is especially true of the large difference in the advertising intensity—a difference of 0.6 percentage points on a base of 1.9 (a 32 percent lift). This difference would translate into millions of dollars spent when applied to individual brands. This is a geared (or magnified) effect that can be illustrated with the following hypothetical example.

> If a brand with a 2 percent share of market accounts for 3.8 percent share of voice in its category, an increase of 32 percent in advertising intensity (from the base of 3.8 percent) lifts its share of voice to 5 percent.
> If the total advertising expenditure in the category is $200 million, the brand's expenditure now totals $10 million, or $2.4 million more than it was originally spending.
> The brand's advertising intensity moves up from 1.9 percent to 2.5 percent.

Table 8.4

Alpha Brands: Quintile Analysis

Quintile	Medium-term share growth/ decline (index)	STAS differential (index)	Advertising intensity (percent)	Price (index)	Promotional intensity (index)
Top (top nine Alpha One)	167	161	3.4	95	116
Second (middle eight Alpha One)	115	144	3.3	97	103
Third (bottom nine Alpha One)	105	134	1.9	105	117
Fourth (top nine Alpha Two)	94	147	2.5	118	117
Bottom (bottom ten Alpha Two)	74	138	1.9	120	110

Another feature of Table 8.3 is the insensitivity of price as an indication of medium-term market place success.

There is more to be found in the data in Table 8.3, and we can get to this by amalgamating all the information from the Alpha One and Alpha Two brands (see Table 7.7 and Table 8.3.). These groups of brands have an essential point in common: They contain only those brands with a positive STAS differential; that is, they all have campaigns that are demonstrably effective in the short term.

The two subgroups of Alpha Two brands form a continuum when added to the three subgroups of Alpha One. All the brands progress upward from the least to the most successful when classified by share change: the least successful being the bottom of Alpha Two and the most successful being the top of Alpha One. Fortuitously, the five groups of brands, all of approximately similar size, make up a quintile analysis covering the range of forty-five Alpha brands. This is a single analysis into five groups of brands, based on their success in the market place measured by medium-term share growth. For each quintile, I have given the average reading for STAS differential, advertising intensity, price, and promotional intensity. These data appear in Table 8.4.

Table 8.5 indexes the figure in each column, the bottom quintile being given the value of 100.

The only marketing input that comes near to predicting the extent of the market share growth is advertising intensity. Quintile by quintile,

Table 8.5

Alpha Brands: Quintile Analysis, Indexed

Quintile	Medium-term share growth/ decline	STAS differ- ential	Advertising intensity	Price	Promo- tional intensity
Top (top nine Alpha One)	226	117	179	79	105
Seond (middle eight Alpha One)	155	104	174	81	94
Third (bottom nine Alpha One)	142	97	100	88	106
Fourth (top nine Alpha Two)	127	106	132	98	106
Bottom (bottom ten Alpha Two)	100	100	100	100	100

advertising intensity and market share growth are much more directly in step than is the case with any of the other inputs. The influence of these stimuli sales in more *geared*—that is, in each case the change in sales is magnified beyond the changes in STAS differential, price, and promotional intensity.

The advertising intensity figures contain one discontinuity, but their direction is clear enough. On the other hand, the rather flatter price trend is continuous. Readers will appreciate that the slope of the price trend is in the opposite direction to the advertising intensity trend, because the greatest sales are associated with the lowest price, but with the highest advertising intensity.

The really striking feature of Table 8.5 is the steepness of the progressions. This represents the strength of the responsiveness of sales to changes in the marketing inputs: increases in advertising pressure and reductions in price. The slopes represent, in rather a crude form, the elasticity—or the degree of sensitivity—of the sales of the Alpha brands to changes in the two stimuli. From Table 8.5, we can calculate the following overall averages, which are of course based on the whole progressive run of forty-five Alpha brands:

Advertising. There is a 79 percent advertising increase (from 100 to 179), associated with a 126 percent share growth (from 100 to 226); these relative amounts of growth are in the ratio of 1.0 to 1.6.

Price. There is a 21 percent price decrease, associated with 126 percent share growth; these relative amounts represent a ratio of 1.0 to 6.0.

Table 8.6

Comparison of Advertising and Price Elasticities

	Published averages: short-term effect	Average of Alpha brands: medium-term effect
Advertising	+0.2	+1.6
Price	−1.8	−6.0

These ratios are the equivalent of a medium-term advertising elasticity of +1.6 percent, and a medium-term price elasticity of −6.0 percent. But the figures are not pure measures because the sales increases are the result of all the inputs working in cooperation with one another.

Nevertheless, these data are rather startling. They are totally out of line with what we know, from the study of other brands, about the responsiveness of sales to changes in advertising pressure and in price. Table 8.6 contains average figures computed from large samples of published cases, and the differences from the Alpha analysis are striking.[2]

What are the reasons for the massive difference in the degree of effect between the Alpha brands and the established averages? There are three interconnected explanations. The first two relate to the advertising elasticity; the third, to advertising and price.

First, there is the distinction between the short- and medium-term effects of the marketing stimuli. There is no dispute that advertising's power to stimulate sales in the short term will generally lead to repeat purchase, which adds a lagged effect to the immediate sales trigger.[3] This explanation partly explains the difference between the two sets of figures, although medium-term effects on their own could not be expected to add all the incremental sales we see in Table 8.6.

The second explanation derives from the fact that the published averages have been computed from a cross-section of brands in many studies, with no attempt to distinguish between the successful and the unsuccessful. In contrast, the Alpha brands are specially selected on the basis of the short-term effectiveness of their advertising campaigns. The average advertising elasticity for all brands, the low figure of +0.2, is a measure that has been pushed down by the nonperformance of the unproductive campaigns. The result for the effective campaigns is likely to be larger, perhaps much larger. However, until now, we have had no way of isolating the productive campaigns from the others.

Figure 8.1   **The Triad of Marketing Stimuli: Three Sources of Synergy**

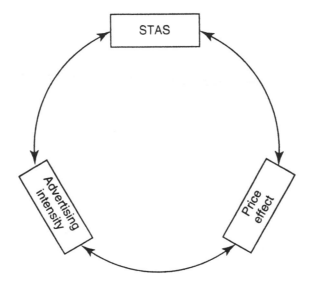

The quintile analysis of the Alpha brands stretches out the range of effects, so that the sales performance of the most efficient campaigns becomes widely separated from that of the least efficient ones. The Alpha One brands have the intrinsic creative strength to boost sales in the short term. They contain a productive engine whose effect is boosted, perhaps multiplied, by media weight. To use the language of this book, media weight prolongs a brand's ups over the course of the year, the effect of which causes the trend line to keep going up.

The first two reasons are reasonably persuasive. But the third reason is the decisively important one.

The published advertising and price elasticities are derived from regression analyses, which isolate the effect of advertising (and not price) and isolate the effect of price (and not advertising). The Alpha brands have not been treated in this way. On the contrary, the various marketing stimuli are seen to be working in conjunction with one another. As we saw in Table 7.5, there is in fact a powerful synergy at work.

The data from the Alpha brands point to the following chain of causality:

1. The STAS differential is larger for the most successful brands.
2. Advertising intensity works on the STAS differential, to generate a first degree of synergy.

Table 8.7

Recommended Advertising Intensity Levels

Market share	Median (percent)	Minimal levels recommended for growth (percent)
1/2/3	3.5	5.0
4/5/6	1.8	3.5
7/8/9	1.2	2.0

3. These two advertising effects now work in cooperation with the price effect, to generate an even more powerful second stage of synergy, as illustrated in Figure 8.1.

Note that the initial impetus comes from the STAS differential, which measures the short-term performance of the advertising. With an effective campaign, synergy is both possible and common although not universal. However, without an effective campaign, synergy is impossible. Advertising intensity is wasted, and the powerful sales potential of price reductions is tamed and muted.

This analysis gives us a clear indication of why the Alpha Two brands have not performed in the long run. The factors that have rendered them ineffective are *too little advertising pressure and too high prices.* And the first of these explanations is the more important one.

Drawing an operational lesson from this conclusion is complicated by the fact that relative media expenditure is invariably governed by the size of the brand. Published aggregated studies demonstrate that the smaller the brand, the higher the share of voice, and the larger the brand, the lower the share of voice. And there is a fairly uniform gradation from small to large brands, with a continuous and progressive decline in share of voice.[4]

This analysis of average shares of voice covers successful and unsuccessful brands. Assessing the optimum advertising intensity for any brand is a judgment call, and each case is conditioned by special circumstances. But in general terms, if a brand is to grow, its campaign should not only produce a positive STAS differential, but also spend at an above-average level. I believe that it should exceed the average for brands of a similar size by a minimum of 0.5 percentage points. For safety, I have rounded this level upward. My specific suggestions can be found in Table 8.7.

The average figures have been extrapolated from the published data to which I have referred and relate to the data in Table 12.1 in Chapter 12 (see page 147). The levels recommended for growth (the right-hand column) are all well above the current levels for the Alpha Two brands.

My hypothesis that the unsuccessful brands pull down the average advertising elasticity level to +0.2 has a parallel with the discussion in Chapter 5. I argued there that a single exposure of a successful campaign will have a positive effect. And I suggested that McDonald's data demonstrating the apparently negative effect of a single exposure were distorted by his being forced to aggregate the successful and unsuccessful campaigns into a single group.

Ten Factors That Account for the Different Sales Performance of the Alpha One and Alpha Two Brands

1. I believe the main factors that transform a short-term campaign effect into a medium-term share improvement are those connected with a brand's advertising. First, there is its STAS differential. Second, there is the brand's advertising intensity, which acts in synergy to prolong and augment advertising's short-term effect (Tables 8.4 and 8.5).
2. Sensitivity to changes in advertising pressure is relevant to the medium-term effects of advertising, not to the short-term ones.
3. Although the advertising inputs are the most important factors affecting share growth for the Alpha brands, there are demonstrable advertising-related scale economies that apply to larger brands. Share of voice tends to be less for larger brands than for smaller ones (Table 8.7). This causes some variation in the importance of advertising within the five quintiles of Alpha brands.
4. Strong synergy exists between the different marketing inputs. Their joint operation boosts the engine of campaign effectiveness (Table 7.5).
5. The greatest influence of low price is its contribution to such synergy. This contribution is driven initially by advertising intensity, working in cooperation with the STAS differential.
6. A lack of advertising intensity prevents the effective campaigns of the Alpha Two brands from driving market share upward in the medium term. The lack of advertising intensity also inhibits the synergy between the different marketing stimuli for these brands.

7. The more a brand is able to maintain the momentum of its positive STAS differential, the greater the relative importance of advertising (Tables 7.9 and 7.10).

8. The more a brand is able to maintain the momentum of its positive STAS differential, the smaller the relative importance of low prices (Tables 7.9 and 7.10).

9. The differences in advertising intensity between the Alpha One and Alpha Two brands appear to be relatively small. However, the advertising intensity levels are geared, so that a difference of a fraction of a percentage point can translate into large dollar sums of advertising investment.

10. Based on the third factor above, I have proposed the levels of advertising intensity necessary to cause sales of Alpha brands to increase, with different suggested levels for brands of different sizes. Each case needs to be judged on its merits, but my proposed rule of thumb is a minimal boost of 0.5 percentage points above the overall average for similar-sized brands. In many cases—for instance, for the Alpha Two brands—this would translate into a significant increase in share of voice and a considerable boost in advertising investment (Table 8.7).

Notes

1. Table 8.1 shows that the Alpha One STAS differential is 43 percent larger than that for the Alpha Two brands (2.0 percentaged on 1.4). This is a weighted calculation. Using the figures in Tables 7.4 and 8.2 gives a smaller difference, but this calculation is based on unweighted numbers.

2. What is known about price elasticities and advertising elasticities is reviewed and discussed in John Philip Jones, "The Double Jeopardy of Sales Promotions," *Harvard Business Review*, September–October 1990, pp. 145–152.

3. Long-term advertising elasticities are discussed in John Philip Jones and Jan S. Slater, *What's in a Name? Advertising and the Concept of Brands* (Armonk, NY: M.E. Sharpe, 2003), pp. 97–100.

4. John Philip Jones, "Ad Spending: Maintaining Market Share," *Harvard Business Review*, January–February 1990, pp. 38–42.

9

Advertising That Works in Some Cases
The Beta Brands

The Beta brands are the twenty largest of the seventy-eight advertising brands studied in this research. I have defined a large brand as one with a market share of 10 percent or more. In the whole field of packaged goods in the United States, such brands represent about one-third of all advertised brands, which means that the sample of large brands in this research is a little below the national average.[1]

Most of my professional life was devoted to large brands, and I gradually learned that they differ from the normal run of brands in more respects than in their size alone. In analyzing large brands, we need to bear in mind six special characteristics, and it is because of these that I decided to separate the large brands in this inquiry and treat them as a special group.

1. Sales of large brands tend to be more sluggish than the general average for all brands. Year by year, their sales do not generally change much, and more than a few large brands have kept their market shares intact for decades. The reason that the share of large brands tends to remain static, and in particular not to increase greatly, is their large volume. An increase of 1 or 2 percent in the sales of a large brand generally means a large and sometimes massive incremental quantity of merchan-

dise, and it is obviously much more difficult to sell this quantity than it is to increase the sales of a small brand by 1 or 2 percent. Selling a given percentage extra gets progressively more difficult as a brand increases in size.

2. Because of the sometimes huge sales volumes of large brands, it is often, if not always, a sign of success for them to hold their current position in the market place, particularly if the category is in decline, for example, cigarettes, coffee, dairy products, and hard liquor. If a brand holds sales in a falling category, its share of market of course goes up.

3. From one point of view, large brands are always under siege. They are invariably the targets of small brands, which are usually launched with the aim of gaining business from subgroups of users of large brands, such as small numbers of consumers who use and enjoy large brands but may be slightly discontented with the price, or the calorie content, or the range of flavors, and so forth. The marketing jargon for this type of competition is the launch of *flanker brands*. (These can either be new brands or variants of existing ones.)

4. Manufacturers of large brands have too often responded to this type of competition by adopting the most dangerous course of action possible, a counterproductive strategy that increases their vulnerability: splintering their large brands into groups of subbrands to cover subcategories of users. In the United States, Coca-Cola now comes in eight separate varieties; Crest toothpaste in twenty-four; Tide powder laundry detergent in six. This type of response is alarming because it causes a breakup of the user base and a loss of scale economies in production and marketing, for example the subdivision of advertising budgets into groups of subbudgets, which are in total less effective than a unified budget for one brand name.[2]

5. The scale economies of large brands are very real. In their application to marketing, such economies stem from certain important characteristics of consumer behavior, and they are expressed by the way in which large brands can use their advertising budgets more productively than small brands can.

A behavioral characteristic distinguishes large brands from small ones: their penetration, or their user base. A large brand has more users than a small brand. However, once a brand exceeds a certain size—normally about a 10 percent share—the brand's purchase frequency also tends to increase over its previous level. People begin to use the brand more often. Some analysts describe this characteristic rather imprecisely as an increase in loyalty to the brand. I prefer to use the less emotive phrase I coined to describe it—the penetration supercharge.[3]

Because consumers are inclined to use large brands rather more often than they use small brands, the advertising for large brands needs to work progressively less hard as a brand gets bigger. The advertising for a large brand becomes more productive than the advertising for a small brand. Hence the phenomenon (discussed more fully in Chapter 12) that the share of voice of small brands tends to be higher than that of large brands, and that share of voice falls progressively as brands get larger.[4]

6. Despite these real advantages, many if not most manufacturers tend to milk (or neglect) their large brands, giving them insufficient attention and resources. In my experience, this has been by far the leading cause of the eventual decline and occasional demise of many large brands. Milking is partly induced by a widespread and dangerous belief in the inevitability of the downward phase of a brand's life cycle. Many—although not all—manufacturers believe that a large brand will erode sooner or later, and they therefore undersupport it because they do not have faith in its future. This policy will of course cause it to lose sales.[5] The reason for withdrawing support is, however, often more pragmatic. Manufacturers set great store by new brand launches, despite the failure of most new brands. All new brand ventures call for major upfront investments in research and development, in production, and in marketing, and these activities are most commonly funded by reductions of support behind existing large brands.[6]

A Bird's-Eye View of the Beta Brands

The details of the individual Beta brands can be seen in Table 9.1. Table 9.2 compares Beta with the average measures for Alpha One and Alpha Two. Table 9.3 compares the trio of market share measures for all three groups of brands.

The Beta brands are not only larger than Alpha One and Alpha Two, but they are also more stable. Moreover, there is evidence of smaller contributions from the various marketing inputs. Although the range of market shares of the Beta brands is very wide—from 10.4 percent to 38.1 percent—the range of the other measures covered in Table 9.1 is remarkably compact. This point is demonstrated in Table 9.4, which examines the spread of the various variables. For instance, the share change for the least successful Beta brand is an index of 85, and for the most

Table 9.1

Beta Brands

Brand	Market share first-quarter 1991 (percent)	Medium-term share growth/ decline (index)	STAS differential (index)	Advertising intensity (percent)	Price (index)	Promotional intensity (index)
CC	10.4	85	89	0.5	114	100
BF	12.3	89	86	0.8	92	82
EB	19.0	89	93	2.5	110	120
CA	15.7	89	98	0.5	117	100
HB	23.6	92	116	1.4	104	131
HC	19.8	92	134	1.1	99	102
AAA	10.9	93	95	1.3	120	94
KAA	13.7	93	109	0.2	121	109
CB	13.3	94	110	0.8	93	77
JB	17.9	95	103	1.3	100	115
KA	22.9	98[a]	96	1.1	118	108
EA	20.9	99[a]	126	1.2	138	97
GB	38.1	101[a]	95	1.4	115	97
AA	16.3	101[a]	97	0.9	131	94
KB	16.9	102[b]	107	1.3	124	105
MA	16.5	110[b]	107	1.1	128	150
HA	25.4	110[b]	117	1.7	110	118
BA	13.8	111[a]	96	1.2	132	101
JA	28.1	114[b]	105	0.9	117	93
DA	16.6	116[b]	122	0.3	52	98
Average	18.6	99	105	1.1	112	105

[a]Advertising effect possible.
[b]Advertising effect probable.

Table 9.2

First Comparison of Averages: Alpha One, Alpha Two, and Beta Brands

Groups	Market share first-quarter 1991 (percent)	Medium-term share growth/ decline (index)	STAS differential (index)	Advertising intensity (percent)	Price (index)	Promotional intensity (index)
Alpha One	3.5	129	147	2.9	99	112
Alpha Two	4.9	83	142	2.2	119	113
Beta	18.6	99	105	1.1	112	105

Table 9.3

Second Comparison of Averages: Alpha One, Alpha Two, and Beta Brands

	Average baseline STAS	Average stimulated STAS	Average achieved market share	Average index of medium-term market share growth/decline
Alpha One	4.0 (= 100)	6.0 (= 150)	4.2 (= 105)	129
Alpha Two	4.5 (= 100)	5.9 (= 131)	4.1 (= 91)	83
Beta	16.7 (= 100)	17.6 (= 105)	18.6 (= 111)	99

Table 9.4

Spread (or Range) of Inputs and Responses for Alpha and Beta Brands

	Alpha One	Alpha Two	Beta
Share change in index points	230	56	31
STAS differential in index points	153	198	48
Advertising intensity in percentage points	8.6	6.0	2.3
Price in index points	111	89	86
Promotional intensity in index points	99	107	73

successful, 116, representing a range or spread of 31 index points. Table 9.4 shows a small spread, demonstrating a rather limited degree of variation brand by brand in comparison with Alpha One and Alpha Two.

The high average price of the Beta brands is evidence both of their endemic strength and high profitability. Users are prepared to pay higher prices for what they perceive to be extra value.

High profitability represents a trade-off for manufacturers. If they choose to stimulate sales more actively than they do at present, the expense of the required price incentives would bite into profitability to such a degree that the extra sales would probably not pay for themselves.[7] The wiser manufacturers (i.e., those who do not neglect their brands) are therefore content to invest enough money in their Beta brands to enable them to make constant sales and steady profits. Remember also the call on manufacturers' resources made by new brand ventures, which are generally accorded preference in investment decisions; this means that manufacturers' attention tends to be drawn away from their large brands.

Nevertheless, some Beta brands do better than others, and I shall at-

Table 9.5

Analysis of Regular and Irregular Users:
Ten Brands of Packaged Detergents

Average STAS differential index	151
STAS differential index: regular users	155
STAS differential index: irregular users	145

tempt to trace the cause. It is a difficult task, because all the measures relating to the Beta brands tend to cluster around the average. There are few extremes in the data to provide diagnostic insights.

The most important point to bear in mind is the one made at the beginning of this chapter: all Beta brands are to some extent under siege. This means that much if not most marketing activity is defensive, and its effectiveness must be judged not so much by its ability to boost share but by its capacity to maintain it or even to slow a decline brought about by continuous competitive pressure.

The Successful and Unsuccessful Beta Brands

Five of the Beta brands are successful for reasons connected with their advertising campaigns: a fact demonstrated by their combination of a positive STAS differential and market share improvement. These brands are marked in Table 9.1 with a superscript [b]. I believe that this total might be increased, and I have added five further brands, marked with a superscript [a]. These show either a constant or an upward share trend, despite a modestly negative STAS differential in four of the five cases.

Why should these last five brands be included as successes, bringing the total of successful Beta brands to ten?[8]

As I have already explained, it is difficult for the Beta brands to grow because of their large size. And when such brands do grow, the growth is the result of increased purchase frequency by existing users rather than of increased penetration (acquiring new users). The evidence from the research in this book is that advertising tends to have a slightly greater effect on regular users than on irregular ones. In my pilot work on the Nielsen data, I made the analysis shown in Table 9.5, which covers the ten advertised brands in the packaged detergents category. In this particular analysis, I defined regular users of any particular brand as users of only one or two brands in the category; irregular users are those who use three or more. I calculated the average STAS differential for each brand for its regular and irregular users separately and then averaged all the figures for the regular and the irregular groups.

The data show that advertising has a slightly greater effect on regular than on occasional users. We should not, however, conclude too much from Table 9.5, because the subsamples from which it was composed are small. But I believe that the direction of the figures is correct. And the regular versus irregular distinction applies to the Beta brands covered by Tables 9.1 and 9.5. Since there is (at least) directional evidence that advertising that works in the short term operates more strongly on regular than occasional users, I believe on judgment that the advertising is working in this way with brands KA, EA, GB, AA, and BA (those marked [a] in Table 9.1), which have at least held their sales or modestly improved them, although their STAS differential shows a small overall reduction in four of the five cases.

If readers accept my conclusion that advertising works effectively for ten of the Beta brands, then the total number of campaigns in this research that are successful in both the short and medium term becomes thirty-six (twenty-six Alpha One plus ten Beta brands). These thirty-six represent (a projected) *46 percent of all advertised brands*, or 25 percent of all brands advertised and unadvertised. The guesses made almost a century ago by William Hesketh Lever and John Wanamaker that half their advertising was wasted may have been slightly optimistic, but they were certainly not wide of the mark. However—rather importantly—we can now identify the half that works and the half that does not.

The Medium-Term Role of Advertising

The most unusual feature of the Beta brands that has emerged from this analysis is their small but uninterrupted improvement in the market share measures (Table 9.3).The Beta brands do not move much, but the short-term campaign effect (+5 percent) is followed by a further progressive improvement over the course of the year (an additional 6 percent). Note that these changes relate to growth of sales from the level of the baseline STAS.[9]

The increase between baseline STAS and achieved market share (a different measure from that used in Table 9.1) is a particularly sensitive indicator of advertising effect, and it suggests that this effect is in line

Table 9.6

Beta Brands: Successful and Unsuccessful Campaigns

	Average market share (percent)	Medium-term share growth/ decline (index)	STAS differ- ential (index)	Advertising intensity (percent)	Price (index)	Promo- tional intensity (index)
Ten successful campaigns	21.6	106	107	1.1	117	106
Ten unsuccessful campaigns	15.7	91	103	1.0	107	103

with the doctrine that advertising works progressively in cooperation with consumer satisfaction with the functional performance of the brand. This is a mutual reinforcement that boosts purchase frequency: a genuinely long-term effect.

The way to test this hypothesis is to examine separately the two groups of Beta brands: those with successful advertising campaigns and those without them. As an aside, it is also interesting to contrast the successful Beta brands (Table 9.6) with the successful Alpha One brands (Table 9.2). The reasons for the success of the Alpha One brands are very clear. It is a more complex procedure to ferret out why the successful Beta brands have actually succeeded.

The most obvious feature of Table 9.6 is the considerable difference between the market share growth of the unsuccessful and successful Beta brands: the latter is 16 percent above the former (106 percentaged on 91). Is this difference caused purely by the greater internal momentum of the successful brands?

Promotions do not appear to be important. And the overall influence of price (which embraces promotions) is nonexistent, since the average price of the more successful brands is 9 percent higher than the less successful ones (117 percentaged on 107). This is a further confirmation of the theory of advertising's long-term effect, just discussed.

We are left with the two advertising-related measures. But the STAS effect is small, and there is no apparent difference in advertising intensity. However, when we consider the latter, we must take into account the average size of the brands. The brands in the successful subgroup are on average 38 percent larger than the unsuccessful ones. The share

Table 9.7

Beta Brands: Advertising/Market Share Matrix

	Unsuccessful brands	Successful brands
Spend above-average for market share	4	8
Spend below-average for market share	6	2[a]

[a]This subgroup contains an exceptional brand, DA, which is driven by low price and is therefore (presumably) forced to cut back its advertising intensity.

of voice of the larger brands should be on average *below* that of the smaller ones. Yet the observed advertising intensity is the same in the two groups. This point needs to be explored, although in doing so we shall be using some small subsamples. In Table 9.7, the average levels of advertising support by which the Beta brands are compared are derived from Table 12.1 in Chapter 12. The data in Table 9.7 are thin. They nonetheless provide some support for the hypothesis that advertising makes a difference to the successful Beta brands. The latter have a slightly higher STAS differential, allied to a greater likelihood of higher effective advertising investment than the unsuccessful Beta brands.

Store Brands

Unadvertised store brands make an instructive comparison with the Beta brands. This research yielded data on nine store brands, although the actual brand names in each product category differed from store to store. This variability does not matter much in this analysis, since there are no advertising-created added values to consider, except for those that are the product of the store's name and reputation, which are the result of broader influences than advertising alone. I shall be concerned essentially with price, and the overall picture of the store brands is shown in Table 9.8.

The number of store brands in my sample (nine out of 142) is below the national average of 20 percent of all brands, representing 15 percent of aggregate dollar market share.[10] (These figures indicate that store brands on average have a dollar share below volume share, which fits with their low prices.) It also suggests that the concentration of this present research on larger brands goes some way to explaining the low representation of store brands.

Table 9.8

Store Brands

Brand	Market share first-quarter 1991 (percent)	Medium-term share growth (index)	Price (index)	Promotional intensity (index)
BQ	3.1	113	72	23
DQ	2.5	116	92	121
EQ	8.1	93	80	53
FQ	41.4	93	82	87
GQ	13.5	100	72	45
HQ	21.7	98	88	51
JQ	6.0	92	79	65
LQ	7.2	104	72	23
MQ	28.9	108	72	78
Average	14.7	102	79	61

In confirmation of this last point, the average market share of the nine store brands is rather lower than that for the Beta brands. The size distribution of the store brands is skewed, with five of them being much below the average. But even with this variability in size, the special situation of store brands, with their guarantee of distribution and display, gives them an internal impetus similar to that enjoyed by the Beta group.

The functional quality of store brands is generally satisfactory, although often a notch below manufacturers' brands. This, together with their distributional strength, provides momentum. The only marketing input that affects them demonstrably is their price. Since promotions play an extremely small role in marketing store brands, their low average cost to the consumer stems from their generally low list prices.

The average rate of growth of store brands is fractionally ahead of the Beta brands. But this progress is paid for by the profit forgone. The expense of manufacturing store brands is probably as a general rule a bit less than that of advertised brands as a consequence of their slightly lower product quality.[11] But their average price is 29 percent below Beta brands (79 compared with 112). It is unlikely that the total advertising investment plus trade promotional allowances of the Beta brands deflate revenue to such an extent. It is therefore reasonably certain that the Beta brands are more profitable to their manufacturers than many if not most store brands. Store brands are also likely to be less profitable to retailers than manufacturers' brands, although the markup may be higher.

Nine Factors That Explain the Performance of the Beta Brands

1. The Beta brands tend to be stable and profitable, as a result of both their large mass and the scale economies they generate.
2. The various marketing inputs play a smaller role with the Beta brands than with Alpha One and Alpha Two.
3. However, the Beta brands are always to some extent under siege, so that they require marketing support for defensive purposes.
4. The Beta brands show on average a positive STAS differential; and half of them boost market share. This progression suggests that the advertising for these brands reinforces the satisfaction felt by existing users and generates increased purchase frequency.
5. Five of the twenty Beta brands have demonstrably effective advertising campaigns. I believe that an additional five brands have campaigns that work in an essentially defensive fashion. Adding the ten effective Beta campaigns to the twenty-six effective Alpha One campaigns gives a total of thirty-six, a (projected) success rate for advertising of 46 percent of advertised brands.
6. The progress of the Beta brands is more a result of their internal momentum than is the case for Alpha One and Alpha Two. Advertising seems to work more as a reinforcement among the Beta group.
7. Promotions have little long-term influence on the Beta brands, and the most successful brands command on average a premium price, which is proof of the high esteem they command from their users.
8. Advertising plays some part in boosting the sales of the successful Beta brands, but the supporting evidence for this claim is thin because of the small sizes of the subsamples.
9. Beta brands bear a resemblance to unadvertised store brands. But since the main engine driving store brands is their low list prices rather than their established strength, store brands will, in many if not most cases, be less profitable than Beta brands, both to the manufacturer and to the storekeeper.

Notes

1. John Philip Jones, *Does It Pay to Advertise? Cases Illustrating Successful Brand Advertising* (New York: Macmillan-Lexington Books, 1989), pp. 300–302.

2. John Philip Jones, *How Much Is Enough? Getting the Most from Your Advertising Dollar* (New York: Macmillan-Lexington Books, 1992), pp. 28–33.

3. John Philip Jones and Jan S. Slater, *What's in a Name? Advertising and the Concept of Brands*, 2nd ed. (Armonk, NY: M.E. Sharpe, 2003), pp. 119, 132.

4. John Philip Jones, "Ad Spending: Maintaining Market Share," *Harvard Business Review*, January–February, 1990, pp. 38–42.

5. Jones, *Does It Pay to Advertise?* Foreword by Sir David Orr.

6. Jones and Slater, *What's in a Name?* pp. 86–90.

7. John Philip Jones, "The Double Jeopardy of Sales Promotions," *Harvard Business Review,* September–October 1990, pp. 145–152.

8. In Chapter 4, I used stricter criteria to identify the brands that should be allowed through the gate to receive further advertising investment. I reduced the ten successful Beta brands to seven, concentrating on those that combined a marginal STAS differential (at least) and premium price. In Chapter 4, I was concentrating on planning for an unknown future. In contrast, Chapter 9 explores the actual experience of the brands, examined post hoc. In these cases, results seem to have been rather better than might have been anticipated.

9. In Table 9.3, the achieved market share is not much different from the first-quarter market share. However the baseline STAS is below the first-quarter market share, and there is an 11 percent rise from baseline STAS to achieved market share. The fact that the first-quarter market share is above the baseline STAS suggests that the positive STAS is actually boosting sales in the first quarter.

10. Emily DeNitto, "Brand Names Learn from Hard Times to Rise Again," *Advertising Age*, April 18, 1994, pp. 3, 46.

11. I certainly found this to be true on many occasions during my professional career.

10

Advertising That Does Not Work
The Gamma Brands

The Gamma brands represent a relatively small group of thirteen names. Their most obvious characteristics can be seen in Table 10.1. They benefit from little share growth overall, although the patterns of increase and decline differ brand by brand. The most important conclusions from Table 10.1 relate to advertising. The short-term advertising strength (STAS) differential shows a reduction from the baseline, averaging 19 percent. This demonstrates that for these brands the short-term effect of advertising is negative: their advertising is not strong enough to prevent a serious loss of business to competitive brands. Yet the advertising intensity of the Gamma brands is higher than that for any of the other groups. Since there is no overall share growth, the relatively high advertising intensity obviously *does not compensate for the lack of advertising quality*.

The weakness in the stimulated STAS and the decline to achieved market share are more pronounced than for any of the other groups of brands (Table 10.2). Note that the baseline STAS (5.5 percent) is significantly higher than the first-quarter market share (4.4 percent in Table 10.1), suggesting that decline was under way from the very beginning of the year.

Measured by the change from first-quarter share to achieved market share, the brands hold their own in total. This overall stability was the end product of increases for some brands and declines for others. But

Table 10.1

Comparison of Averages: Alpha One, Alpha Two, Beta, and Gamma Brands

	Market share first-quarter 1991 (percent)	Medium-term share growth/ decline (index)	STAS differ-ential (index)	Advertising intensity (percent)	Price (index)	Promotional intensity (index)
Alpha One	3.5	129	147	2.9	99	112
Alpha Two	4.9	83	142	2.2	119	113
Beta	18.6	99	105	1.1	112	105
Gamma	4.4	103	81	3.3	115	107

since the advertising had no short-term effect, some other dynamics must be at work to boost the more successful brands. Yet the Gamma brands in general are neither underpriced nor overpromoted (Table 10.1). We must therefore look at the performance of individual brands for clues to why the more successful ones succeeded.

Table 10.3 describes the individual brands that make up the Gamma group. This table has a number of interesting features.

- The brands are almost evenly split between those that lost market share and those that gained. This range of the changes is reasonably large, from –23 percent to +35 percent.
- The STAS differentials are all negative, with some skew in their distribution, four brands being below the Gamma mean and nine brands above it.
- As mentioned, the average advertising intensity is high, 3.3 percentage points, although the distribution is again skewed, with nine brands below the Gamma mean and four brands above it. The overall range is exceptionally wide, from 0.1 to 14.2 percentage points.
- The average price of the Gamma brands is 15 percent above their category average, and eight of the brands are in turn higher than the Gamma average. The relatively high (effective) prices are a reflection of high list prices. This factor imposes a general brake on the Gamma brands.
- Average promotional intensity of the Gamma brands is 7 percent above their category average. Promotions do not have enough weight to compensate for the high list prices.

Table 10.2

Alpha One, Alpha Two, Beta, and Gamma:
Trio of Market Share Measures

	Average baseline STAS	Average stimulated STAS	Average achieved market share	Medium-term share growth/ decline (index)
Alpha One	4.0 (= 100)	6.0 (= 150)	4.2 (= 105)	129
Alpha Two	4.5 (= 100)	5.9 (= 131)	4.1 (= 91)	83
Beta	16.7 (= 100)	17.6 (= 105)	18.6 (= 111)	99
Gamma	5.5 (= 100)	4.3 (= 78)	4.5 (= 82)	103

Table 10.3

Gamma Brands

	Market share first- quarter 1991 (percent)	Medium- term share growth/ decline (index)	STAS differ- ential (index)	Advertising intensity (percent)	Price (index)	Promotional intensity (index)
CO	3.0	77	94	1.0	117	136
BEE	3.5	80	67	3.1	120	120
KE	3.9	87	82	1.8	98	96
BN	6.4	89	93	3.9	119	113
DJ	2.8	97	84	1.1	68	133
KF	3.2	97	83	1.2	106	106
KBB	7.8	105	91	0.1	118	118
LA	5.3	109	85	1.9	64	108
EF	6.0	112	97	2.3	104	89
FA	7.7	114	44	3.5	128	125
MD	3.1	119	81	2.9	137	67
FE	2.6	123	76	14.2	147	105
DL	1.7	135	75	5.9	165	80
Average	4.4	103	81	3.3	115	107

- The Gamma brands are different from the Alpha One and Alpha Two in that there is no decline from the level of the stimulated STAS to achieved market share (Table 10.2). Since there is a pronounced dip from baseline STAS to stimulated STAS, there are no temporary sales increases to erode. And—unlike the Beta brands— there are no small temporary increments on which to build.

Table 10.4

Increasing and Declining Gamma Brands

Brands	Market share first-quarter 1991 (percent)	Average medium-term share growth/ decline (index)	Average STAS differential (index)	Advertising intensity (percent)	Price (index)	Average promotional intensity (index)
Top seven	4.9	117	78	4.4	123	99
Bottom six	3.8	88	84	2.0	105	117

Why Are Some Gamma Brands Successful?

In the same way that I divided the Alpha One, Alpha Two, and Beta brands into subgroups, Table 10.4 divides the Gamma brands. The sample size of thirteen is unfortunately small, but there is a clear dividing line: between the subgroup of seven brands that are increasing and the six that are declining.

Table 10.4 has one very puzzling feature. The theory of advertising used in this book, consistently supported by the data for the Alpha One, Alpha Two, and Beta brands, holds that the sales effect of advertising is triggered by the STAS differential and prolonged and augmented by advertising intensity. The theory also predicates that a negative STAS differential, showing a clear absence of short-term sales effect, is incapable of boosting sales in the medium term. However, the data from Table 10.4 show that the most successful Gamma brands are more advertising-intensive than the less successful ones, contradicting this theory. The more successful Gamma brands appear to show that advertising is capable of a medium-term effect without an initial short-term trigger.

However, there is one fact that denies this possibility. During 1992, only two of the seven growing Gamma brands continued to increase. If the growth of these brands during 1991 is a signal of medium-term effect in the absence of short-term effect, why did this medium-term stimulus not continue after the end of the year? There must be other factors that have caused the growth during 1991. In fact, I believe that certain of the Gamma brands have special features and that we can find other ways of explaining the sales increase of the top seven brands.

One brand (LA) is driven by an exceptionally low list price: the bottom (relative) price in the Gamma group. This is the obvious reason for LA's success in 1991; nevertheless, the brand declined in 1992.

Two brands (KBB and DL) have highly visible brand names because they are line extensions of other ubiquitous and successful products: either in the same category (KBB) or in a related category (DL). Sales success was due to a rub-off from the established and successful brands to the two Gamma brands. However, this factor was not strong enough to maintain the sales increase in 1992.

Three of the apparently successful Gamma brands are widely familiar because of their long history and prominence in the market place, which I believe to be greater than their sales levels suggest (EF, FA, and MD). In my opinion, the apparent buoyancy of these brands was partly the result of their "living off their fat." The identity of their manufacturers also suggests that these brands received substantial trade promotional support. The advertising budgets of all three of these brands were deployed in an extremely unusual fashion: they were concentrated strongly into one-quarter of the year. However, there is no evidence of extra sales in the periods of advertising concentration, suggesting that the brands were insensitive to changes in advertising pressure. Interestingly enough, two of these three brands were soon in trouble. The sales of EF went down in 1992 and the brand was withdrawn from the market in 1993. FA (whose sales went up in 1992) was sold as a complete entity to another manufacturer.

One brand (FE) has a freak advertising intensity figure of 14.2 percentage points. This reading actually distorts the average advertising intensity for the top seven Gamma brands. FE ran advertising that produced an unusual effect. The campaign won creative prizes and was used to persuade the retail trade to accept the brand, which had been sold in only one part of the United States. Therefore, although the advertising had no effect on the consumer, it helped greatly to extend the geographical area of the brand's retail distribution, and this is what pushed up its sales. (The manufacturer of FE and his advertising agency recognized their brand from the figures published in the first edition of this book, and I was invited to attend a meeting with them to discuss my findings.)

I believe overall that, although the Gamma brands do not provide positive support for my explanation of medium-term effects they do not negate that theory. Most of the growing Gamma brands do not have any prolonged sales success, and the progress of a number of them in 1991 can be explained by reasons unconnected with the advertising.

Five Reasons That Explain the Performance of the Gamma Brands

1. The negative STAS differential of all the Gamma brands exerts a downward pressure, and for six of the thirteen brands, there are no forces to counter it.
2. The Gamma brands are on average priced relatively high, and this acts as a brake on growth. However, individual brands are stimulated to low prices or high promotional intensity.
3. The market place performance of some Gamma brands raises the possibility that their sales success could be the product of high-advertising intensity, despite the negative STAS. This suggests that advertising might work in the medium term without any initial short-term impetus. But this possibility is denied by the experience of 1992. Most of the growing Gamma brands *did not continue to increase* in 1992. And an examination of the individual brands suggests special reasons for the increases in 1991.
4. Since advertising has little influence on the Gamma brands, which are also priced rather high, there is no synergy between effective advertising and the low prices.
5. The Gamma brands are stagnant overall. Half are declining, mainly because of deficient advertising quality. The increases in the remaining Gamma brands are driven by stimuli other than advertising.

— 11 —

Penetration and Purchase Frequency

This chapter has two objectives. It is written to remind advertising practitioners that:

1. Advertising is predominantly concerned with consumer behavior. And although advertising is capable of affecting such behavior significantly, it tends to be impeded in any attempt to *change* behavior by the innate uniformity and regularity of purchasing patterns. These are described in this chapter.
2. When a brand becomes established and joins the homemaker's repertoire, this uniformity or regularity of purchasing patterns contributes to maintaining the brand's position in the repertoire. The role of advertising therefore becomes increasingly protective and reinforcing. It aims to boost purchase frequency, not penetration.

The normal way of monitoring the effect of advertising is by measuring the sales of the advertised brand: through retail stores or alternatively as brands enter the home. Yet there is no direct link between advertising and those sales, because advertising is addressed to consumers, and a number of factors can impede advertising's ability to induce consumers to act. It can be countered by the efforts of competitive brands, there may be large stocks of the brand in the home to absorb any

Table 11.1

Sales and Consumer Behavior

Sales of a brand in a defined period = Household population (A)
× Penetration (B)
× Purchase frequency (C)
× Packs bought per purchase occasion (D)
× Average size of pack (E)

increased demand, and the brand may not achieve full retail distribution so that the consumer's effort to buy it is frustrated. To dig out what advertising is actually accomplishing, we should therefore look not only at sales, but also at measures of how advertising affects the underlying aspects of consumer behavior that govern sales.

The relationship between sales and the key measures of consumer behavior is expressed in a simple formula, which we see in Table 11.1. This formula, together with the other analyses in this chapter, is based on the methods first developed by the British mathematician Andrew Ehrenberg, who has worked with large accumulations of data from the United States and a number of other countries.[1] (This formula is revisited in Appendix A.)

When we compare different brands in any product category using the formula in Table 11.1, we find no important differences as far as measures A, D, and E are concerned. The household population—whose buying would represent the strictly theoretical upper limit to any brand's sales—is the same for every national brand. People tend to purchase the same number of packs on every occasion, no matter what brand in the category they may be buying. And the packs of different brands are generally sold in more or less uniform sizes.[2]

We can therefore conclude that the sales of any brand in a defined period are determined by the brand's penetration, which is a measure of the number of buyers who buy it at least once, and its purchase frequency, which measures how often they buy it in the period we are looking at. In this research, these two variables are measured in the following ways.

Penetration covers the full year 1991. When we measure penetration, there is an important technical reason for specifying the time period. A brand's penetration tends to be the same when measured in any individual periods of equal length, for example, January, February, or March. But as the time period itself is extended, penetration goes up: it is higher in all of

1991 than in January of 1991 alone. Penetration grows because some buy-ers buy the brand for the first time during each period. However, new buyers dwindle in numbers in succeeding periods, because increasing numbers of them have in fact bought the brand some time in the past; in other words, they are really infrequent buyers rather than new buyers. This factor causes penetration to grow, but at a declining rate.

On the other hand, market share does not change greatly as the period is lengthened. When we extend the period, total category sales and sales of any particular brand increase approximately in step, so that the ratio between the two—which is the brand's market share—remains relatively constant. Market share in all of 1991 is approximately the same as in January 1991.

Purchase frequency is based on volume sales per buyer. Since vol-ume sales differ by category (not to speak of the differences between categories in the units used to measure sales), I have based the calcula-tion on the category itself, by indexing each brand's volume sales per buyer on the average sales of all brands in its category. I call this calcu-lation the purchase frequency index.[3]

Penetration and purchase frequency are significant measures, for two separate reasons. First, their relative importance varies according to the size of the brand, which means that their relevance to advertising strat-egy is determined to a large degree by market share. The most common example of this variation is that small brands are normally driven by a penetration-based strategy, while large brands are much more directed toward increasing purchase frequency.

The second reason for the importance of penetration and purchase frequency is that they are closely related to three further measures of consumer behavior: the frequency distribution of purchases, the pat-terns of repeat purchase, and multibrand buying. There are regular and uniform relationships whose very consistency has enabled them to be modeled mathematically. This was part of Ehrenberg's groundbreaking work. His models were derived from a broad range of empirical data and were rooted in penetration and purchase frequency. However, the data in this chapter show that detectable changes have taken place since Ehrenberg made his original calculations. (Much of his information dates from before 1970.)

It is unnecessary to explain Ehrenberg's models in this chapter. How-ever, I shall make a few comparisons between my findings and Ehrenberg's *observed* data (not the predictions of his models).

Table 11.2

**All Brands in Quintiles According to Market Share:
Penetration and Purchase Frequency**

Quintile	Average market share (percent)	Average penetration (percent)	Purchase frequency (index)
First	1.8	6.3	84
Second	2.8	7.7	94
Third	3.9	11.0	92
Fourth	6.8	18.6	97
Fifth	18.7	26.9	125

Table 11.3

All Brands: Market Share-to-Penetration Ratios

Quintile	Penetration (market share = 100)
First	350
Second	275
Third	282
Fourth	273
Fifth	144

The 142 brands covered in this research are analyzed in Table 11.2. I have made a quintile analysis by ranking these brands by market share, based on their sales over the full year 1991.[4] This method makes for a proper comparison with the penetration figures for the same period. The quintiles range from the smallest brands (first quintile) to the largest (fifth quintile).

The penetration growth is plotted in Figure 11.1. Here, penetration and market share are seen to progress upward together, showing that sales growth is essentially a function of growth in the numbers of buyers of a brand. However, Figure 11.1 also shows that the growth of penetration takes place at a declining rate as brands get bigger (for reasons already explained).

The decline in the rate of increase of penetration is demonstrated in Table 11.3, which calculates the ratios of market share to penetration. In this table, we can see a sharp decline for the biggest brands.

Since penetration growth becomes less important as a brand increases

Figure 11.1 **Relationship Between Share of Market and Penetration:
Brands in Twelve Categories**

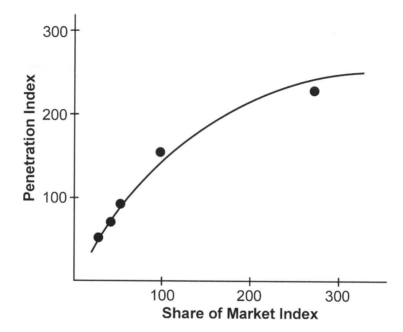

in share, the largest brands must obviously be driven by something else—
increased purchase frequency. This is clear from Table 11.2, which shows
that the major increase in purchase frequency takes place in the fifth
quintile. And if we look exclusively at the figures for the twenty-five
brands with a market share of 10 percent or more (the twenty Beta brands
plus five unadvertised large brands), the purchase frequency index becomes even higher, at 127.

These data demonstrate an important aspect of the penetration supercharge, which was discussed in connection with the Beta brands in Chapter 9. As explained there, the growth of small brands is most strongly
associated with increasing penetration, and purchase frequency does not
change much as a brand grows to an approximate 10 percent share of
market. But when it gets to this level, its increased penetration is accom-
panied by a measurable step-up in its purchase frequency. People begin
to buy the brand more often, primarily as a result of satisfaction with the
brand's functional properties, operating in conjunction with the added
values nurtured by advertising.

This process causes the pace of the brand's internal momentum to be

Table 11.4

Brand Groups: Penetration and Purchase Frequency

	Number of brands	Average market share (percent)	Average penetration (percent)	Purchase frequency (index)
Unadvertised	64	5.5	9.9	103
Alpha One	26	4.0	14.6	82
Alpha Two	19	4.4	12.0	89
Beta—successful	10	22.6	31.8	130
Beta—unsuccessful	10	14.7	26.1	121
Gamma	13	4.5	14.2	81

Table 11.5

Brand Groups: Market Share-to-Penetration Ratios

	Penetration (market share = 100)
Unadvertised	180
Alpha One	365
Alpha Two	272
Beta—growing	141
Beta—declining	178
Gamma	315

increased, and an important result is that the brand's advertising *does not need to work as hard to maintain or boost sales.* Hence, a brand's share of voice tends to decline as its market share increases.

These facts about penetration and purchase frequency help us understand the reasons for the progress in the market place of the seventy-eight advertised and sixty-four other brands covered in this research. The basic data appear in Table 11.4, and in Table 11.5 I have calculated the ratios of market share to penetration.

We can draw three clear conclusions plus one speculative one from Tables 11.4 and 11.5.

1. The successful (but relatively small) Alpha One brands are driven by penetration, their ratio of market share to penetration being higher than for any other group. In comparison with Alpha One, the Alpha Two brands show a lower market share-to-penetration ratio—a reflection of their lack of staying power, their inability to maintain the impetus of their positive STAS differential.

2. The Beta brands have a purchase frequency much above the average, and for the successful Beta brands it is higher still. This demonstrates that the driving force for these brands comes essentially from increased purchasing by existing buyers.

3. The unadvertised brands have a much lower penetration than any of the groups of advertised brands. This is negative confirmation that advertising is a driving force for penetration (for all except the largest brands).

4. The fourth, and more speculative, conclusion from Tables 11.4 and 11.5 relates to the puzzling features of the unsuccessful group of Gamma brands. What caused their relatively high market share-to-penetration ratio of 315? The Gamma brands, like the Alpha One brands, are relatively small, which suggests that the share-to-penetration ratio for the two groups might be broadly similar. But the argument in Chapter 10 raises an additional possibility. I believe that those Gamma brands that increased their sales were driven by forces *other than their advertising*, and these forces are likely to have boosted their penetration and purchase frequency. On the other hand, the declining Gamma brands have figures below the Gamma average: a penetration of 10.2 percent and a purchase frequency index of 75. The successful and unsuccessful Gamma brands are therefore averaged out in Table 11.4.

Frequency Distribution of Purchases

Analysts have known for decades that consumer purchasing in all categories of repeat-purchase packaged goods is skewed, with heavy buyers accounting for a disproportionately high percentage of sales volume. This concentration is normally expressed as the 80:20 rule, which describes an approximation of the average buying distribution: the 80 percent of lightest buyers and the 20 percent of heaviest buyers of any brand each account for 50 percent of its sales.[5] The data from the present investigation show that in most cases, the degree of concentration of purchasing has increased since the 80:20 averages were originally estimated.[6] In Table 11.6, I have computed the share of purchases accounted for by the top 20 percent of buyers in each product category. In Table 11.7, I have analyzed the brands by groups.

Most of the figures in Table 11.6 are marginally below those in Table

Table 11.6

Product Categories: Frequency Distribution of Purchases of Average Brands (in percent)

Category	Proportion of purchases accounted for by 20 percent of heaviest buyers
Packaged detergents	53
Liquid detergents	54
Bar soaps	50
Shampoos	53
Toilet tissue	46
Ice cream	58
Mayonnaise	52
Peanut butter	55
Ground coffee	55
Diet carbonated soft drinks	67
Breakfast cereals	52
Analgesics	59

Table 11.7

Brand Groups: Frequency Distribution of Purchases of Average Brands (in percent)

	Proportion of purchases accounted for by 20 percent of heaviest buyers
Unadvertised	57
Alpha One	59
Alpha Two	57
Beta	60
Gamma	60

11.7, because Table 11.6 includes the substantial numbers of All Others —brands that are individually not significant and not listed. Table 11.7 gives a truer picture of the frequency distribution of the most substantial and better-established brands, whether or not they are advertised. Table 11.7 shows clearly that the proportion of volume accounted for by heavy users has increased from the traditional 50 percent to almost 60 percent. And there is no reason to expect that the trend toward even greater concentration will reverse course in the future.

The advertising strategy for any brand normally embraces two objectives, although the relative weight given to each will differ brand by brand: first, to increase penetration (especially important for small brands), and second, to increase purchase frequency by light users (particularly important for large brands).

The facts about frequency distribution suggest that all manufacturers should reconsider the balance between an offensive strategy (i.e., increasing business) and a defensive one (i.e., defending existing business). The facts about frequency distribution and the probability that present trends will continue apply to all brands, large and small. This strongly suggests that *protection of the franchise should play a larger role* in advertising than it appears to do in most cases today. Advertisers should remember that it is always a poor exchange to acquire as many as four new (light) users, if the price of this gain is the loss of even one existing (heavy) user.

The highest concentration ratios are mainly a result of past increases in purchase frequency for larger brands. This is certainly true of the diet carbonated soft drinks category and also of the Beta brands generally.

Repeat Buying

The rate of repeat buying for any brand is connected with the growth in its penetration. When we compare periods that follow each other, the proportion of buyers of any brand in the first period who will buy it again in the next period is remarkably uniform. The only qualification to this generalization is that the periods measured must be of equal length. The data in this chapter are quarterly figures, averaged across 1991. The repeat purchase rates for the different product categories are detailed in Table 11.8 and for the different brand groups in Table 11.9.

Note three features of Tables 11.8 and 11.9:

1. Although there are variations in repeat purchase rates between product categories, the rates are 33 percent or more in every product category except shampoos, which operate in a crowded and hypercompetitive environment.
2. Surprisingly, the repeat buying rates are below the levels calculated by Ehrenberg, whose average quarterly repeat rates were mostly around 60 percent.[7] Ehrenberg's figures are illustrative and based on a small sample of brands; they may therefore not have been intended to describe general patterns. There is nevertheless quite a large difference between Ehrenberg's figures and mine. The only reason that occurs to me for the apparent lower-

Table 11.8

Product Categories: Repeat Buying Rates of Average Brands (in percent)

Category	Proportion of purchasers in first period who repeat in second period
Packaged detergents	38
Liquid detergents	36
Bar soaps	40
Shampoos	27
Toilet tissue	50
Ice cream	48
Mayonnaise	46
Peanut butter	41
Ground coffee	55
Diet carbonated soft drinks	51
Breakfast cereals	47
Analgesics	33

Table 11.9

Brand Groups: Repeat Buying Rates of Average Brands (in percent)

	Proportion of purchasers in first period who repeat in second period
Unadvertised	39
Alpha one	40
Alpha two	37
Beta	49
Gamma	41

ing of the average repeat rates over the past two decades is that the more recent figures are connected with the increases in the concentration ratios (Tables 11.6 and 11.7). Since the light users, who represent 80 percent of purchasers, now account for a lower proportion of any brand's volume than in the past, it seems likely that their repeat purchase rates have fallen and brought down the averages.

3. The high figure for repeat purchase of the Beta brands fits with the high purchase frequency of these brands. Table 11.9 therefore demonstrates a second manifestation of the penetration supercharge. Not only do buyers of large brands buy them more often in a given period (Table 11.4), but the repeat buying rate from period to period is also higher (Table 11.9).

Table 11.10

Brand Repertoire: Deal and Nondeal Purchases (in percent)

	Packaged detergents			
	Buyers (add down)	Purchases (add down)	Deal purchases (add across)	Nondeal purchases (add across)
Total	100	100	38	62
Buyers of				
One brand	33	18	28	72
Two brands	24	20	29	71
Three brands	14	16	37	63
Four brands	11	13	43	57
Five brands	6	10	39	61
Six brands or more	12	23	53	47

The actual relationship between repeat buying and penetration can be easily explained. Readers will remember that, in periods of the same length, a brand's penetration tends to remain constant. But as the measurement period is extended, penetration goes up. If in the first period the penetration of a brand is indexed at 100, a 40 percent repeat rate means that 40 percent of buyers carry over into the next period. The second period's penetration (the same level as in the first period) is therefore made up of 40 percent repeaters and 60 percent new buyers. The penetration in the first period was 100: the penetration in the first and second periods together is therefore now 160 (100 from the first period plus the 60 percent of new buyers in the second period).

As a specific example of this calculation, the quarterly penetration of Brand AA was 31 percent. With a repeat purchase rate of 41 percent, the brand's net penetration in two quarters was boosted to 49 percent (31 plus 18, which is 59 percent of 31).

Multibrand Buying

Multibrand buying applies generally to all product categories, and the number of buyers of two or more brands almost always exceeds the numbers of buyers of one brand (a group known as solus buyers). The basic data collected in this research are set out in Table 11.10. The figures relate to the full year 1991. The phrase *brand repertoire* is used to describe the number of brands (sometimes also the names of the actual brands) bought by the consumer.

Table 11.11

Composition of the Brand Repertoire (in percent)

	One brand		Two brands		Three or more brands	
	Buyers percent (add across)	Purchases percent (add across)	Buyers percent (add across)	Purchases percent (add across)	Buyers percent (add across)	Purchases percent (add across)
Packaged detergents	33	18	24	20	43	62
Liquid detergents	38	17	23	20	39	63
Bar soaps	30	17	25	20	45	63
Shampoos	33	12	24	17	43	71
Toilet tissue	18	11	16	12	66	77
Ice cream	31	15	28	22	41	63
Mayonnaise	55	39	31	36	14	25
Peanut butter	48	31	30	30	22	39
Ground coffee	32	15	22	19	46	66
Diet carbonated soft drinks	24	6	19	10	57	84
Breakfast cereals	6	1	7	2	87	97
Analgesics	43	23	29	29	28	48

Table 11.10 gives fuller details of one typical product category: packaged detergents. This table breaks down the deal and nondeal purchases for buyers of different numbers of brands. As expected, buyers of many different brands tend to be more deal-driven than buyers of only a few. This applies with appropriate corrections to all categories. Ehrenberg has shown that existing buyers of a brand will take up most of the price promotions for it. Therefore, people who buy many brands will be buyers of large amounts of promoted merchandise.

In Table 11.11, the proportions of buyers and the number of their purchases are reasonably consistent across product categories, although four of the twelve categories show more extreme figures—toilet tissue and breakfast cereals with a wider brand repertoire and mayonnaise and peanut butter with a narrower one.

One aspect of the data demonstrates a change since Ehrenberg made his estimates of average patterns. As we saw with quarterly repeat purchase rates, Ehrenberg's figures are illustrative and based on a small sample of brands: therefore they are probably not intended to describe general averages. Nevertheless, there are again quite large differences between Ehrenberg's figure and mine. My 1991 figures show that solus

Table 11.12

Duplication of Purchase: Proportion of Buyers of First Brand Who Also Buy Second Brand (in percent)

Second brand	First brand					Average 14 brands
	CC	CD	CE	CF	CG	
CC	100	23	22	21	23	24
CD	26	100	27	31	35	32
CE	15	16	100	19	23	17
CF	14	18	18	100	18	17
CG	13	17	18	15	100	16

usage is now common, at levels ranging from 6 percent to 55 percent, with a median about 33 percent. Ehrenberg's average (for a forty-eight-week period) was 12 percent.[8] The reasons for the apparent increase in solus buying are not entirely clear, but there is presumably a connection with the increased concentration of purchasing among the heaviest 20 percent of buyers (Tables 11.6 and 11.7).

Multibrand buying is a relatively consistent phenomenon, with one surprising aspect. There is a way of predicting what other brands are also bought by users of any particular brand in a category. If we go through the laborious exercise of estimating how many buyers of one brand will also buy other identified brands, the patterns that emerge are illustrated in the matrix in Table 11.12. In this table I have stripped down the data to five brands in the bar soap category. I chose these brands and this category arbitrarily (my pilot work was confined to this product category).

The first horizontal line of figures shows the percentages of users of the first brand (also listed horizontally) who use CC: 23 percent of users of CD use CC; 22 percent of users of CE use CC; 21 percent of users of CF use CC, and soon. There is a degree of uniformity in the horizontal lines of figures, and these are averaged in the last vertical column (the averages include all the brands in the category, not just the five itemized in Table 11.12). The first figure in the right-hand column (24 percent) is the average number of users of each brand who also use CC; the second figure (32 percent) is the average number of users of each brand who use CD, and so on. Each figure in the right-hand column is related to the penetration of the second brand to which it refers, in fact a multiple of it. The right-hand column figure for CC is 24 percent and CC's penetration

Table 11.13

Duplication of Purchase Coefficients

Packaged detergents	1.9
Liquid detergents	2.6
Bar soaps	1.2
Shampoos	1.7
Toilet tissue	1.2
Ice cream	1.2
Mayonnaise	1.6
Peanut butter	1.0
Ground coffee	2.0
Diet carbonated soft drinks	1.9
Breakfast cereals	1.4
Analgesics	1.2

is 20 percent. Its multiple is 1.2, a figure known as the duplication of purchase coefficient.[9]

By multiplying a brand's penetration by its duplication of purchase coefficient, we can estimate the proportion of buyers of any other brand in the category who will buy that brand. The category averages of the duplication of purchase coefficients are set out in Table 11.13. There are differences from category to category, but all the coefficients are of a similar order of magnitude.

The Long-Term Effect of a Brand's Internal Momentum

In my discussion of how advertising works in Chapter 5, I made the following points:

In the short term, successful advertising is mainly driven by STAS, which is a measure of the creative effectiveness of the advertising campaign. The media selection and the budgetary weight do not play an important part at this stage. An initial STAS effect is a requirement for a medium-term effect. A strong STAS differential does not guarantee a medium-term effect, but such an effect is impossible without one.

In the medium term, STAS continues to play a role but it is joined by two additional factors. All three, working in cooperation with one another, sometimes manage to generate a strong and economic driving force that strengthens over time. The three factors are:

1. The continuation of the STAS effect.

2. Media continuity, which ensures that the brand has as many short-term ups as possible, to fight and neutralize the pressures of competitive brands. Media continuity depends on both the size of the advertising budget and the method by which it is deployed. This means that, within the individual flights, there must be enough concentration to ensure that most members of the target group are exposed to one advertisement for the brand weekly. Given this proviso, the advertising must then be spread over as many weeks of the year as the budget will allow.

3. The brand's internal momentum. The strength and durability of this is governed by consumer satisfaction with the brand's functional properties and whether they are in harmony with its nonfunctional added values, which are in turn both created and nurtured by advertising. Repeat purchase and added values resonate with each other to produce an incremental effect. This is measured by the proven ability of large brands to be supported with a share of voice that declines progressively as market share increases. It also explains why brands that are rich in added values are so often able to command a premium price.

This book has dealt fully with the first two of these factors. There is, however, information in the present chapter that can both illuminate and confirm the effectiveness of a brand's internal momentum.

Let me reiterate the point—which I believe to be essentially true—that this momentum is driven by the brand as a whole and in particular by consumers' continuous experience of it, and not solely by the lagged effect of previous advertising. In my view, the latter is relevant only to the degree by which it has influenced the brand in the past. I am therefore extremely skeptical of the value of any measurement of the supposed long-term effect of advertising alone, especially when the measuring is done by monitoring consumer perceptions, with all the intrinsic difficulties of that procedure: for example, some campaigns can be much more easily recalled than others because of the creative styles.[10]

This present chapter amplifies and supports the theory of internal momentum in at least ten ways:

1. Small brands are driven by penetration because the STAS effect attracts new users. Assuming that the brand is functionally dis-

tinctive and satisfies consumers, the brand now begins to develop an internal momentum, whose real payoff is in the long term.

2. The double evidence that most users buy more than one brand in any category and that duplication of purchase between all brands in a category is to be expected and can be calculated underscores the importance of a brand's functional qualities. These have to be kept up to date and competitive. Consumers compare brands and will discard unsatisfactory brands without any compunction at all.

3. The evidence that the largest brands benefit not only from higher penetration but also from greater purchase frequency than small brands demonstrates the increasing momentum that can be generated by repeat purchase. This represents a scale economy of large brands. The fact that larger brands can be supported by a lower share of voice than small brands demonstrates that advertising and repeat purchase, and the demonstrably increasing productivity of this cooperation, are the first and most important manifestation of the penetration supercharge.

4. The skewed distribution of purchase frequency, and in particular the large and probably increasing share of purchases accounted for by the 20 percent of heaviest buyers, are evidence of the cumulative effect of the internal momentum of the more durable brands. These are mostly, but not all, large brands. Directing part of every brand's advertising to protecting the high purchase frequency of heavy users is an important means of maintaining a brand's internal momentum.

5. The higher level of repeat buying of the Beta brands is an additional manifestation of the penetration supercharge.

6. The growth during the past two decades in the proportion of solus buyers provides supporting evidence for the internal momentum of those brands that consumers use exclusively.

7. The most striking characteristic of the analyses of the frequency distribution of purchases and of repeat and multibrand buying is *regularity*. There is no way in which the patterns in Tables 11.6 through 11.13 could be haphazard. But it is a difficult matter to explain the reason for such regularity. The only sensible conclusion we can draw—and it is admittedly unoriginal—is that consumer preferences in the population constitute a complex web that is the unconscious product of the activities of

manufacturers in the past, who were responsible for the construction of today's product categories. Choice of brands is governed by these preferences, which cannot be articulated even by the consumers who determine them. The resulting patterns are pronounced, consistent with one another, and slow to change. The best rationalization for these uniform patterns is that buying is governed to a profound degree by habit. This is important to manufacturers for two reasons.

8. The first reason is that it is very hard to break consumers' habits, which explains the widely appreciated difficulty of launching successful new brands.[11] The major problem is not so much the initial launch, which may make short-term, temporary progress. A strong manufacturer can force—or buy—retail distribution. Consumer sampling can be carried out fairly easily through promotions. And advertising campaigns with a positive STAS differential are not uncommon. The real difficulty of launching successful new brands lies in building the right combination of functional rewards and added values—a salient combination for consumers that will start to build an internal momentum. The intractability of this task is the probable reason why at least 90 percent of new brands fail.

9. The second reason why the strength of consumer habits is very important to manufacturers is that habit represents a positive quality that becomes very valuable to successful and established brands. A brand's internal momentum, as it generates drive, eventually achieves what seems to be the opposite effect: it builds consumer inertia. The brand will now be bought as part of an unthinking process, stubbornly remaining in the homemaker's repertoire and resisting the assaults of aggressive new brands. Brands have been known to maintain modest places in the homemaker's repertoire for years, sometimes even for decades, after advertising support has been withdrawn. Manufacturers are, however, generally unconscious of the cost of such an operation: the profit they forgo by the price incentives necessary to keep unadvertised brands in distribution in the retail trade. (See the data on unadvertised brands in Chapter 2 and on store brands in Chapter 9).

10. The last point in this chapter is the most important one. Manufacturers who are educated into the unyielding and uniform pat-

terns of consumer purchasing may be led to believe that change is impossible. They risk adopting a frame of mind that can best be described as catatonic. They will become mute, passive, and unwilling to take action, effective or ineffective. The reality of markets is that, despite their apparent stability, they are actually kept in balance by the opposing aggressive actions of competitors: actions that end up by being substantially self-canceling. For manufacturers to protect their position, they have to act with determination, although their only reward may be the maintenance of the status quo. But for any manufacturer to grow, the qualities needed today—as in the past—are superior resources, persistence, aggressiveness, imagination, and brains.

Notes

1. A.S.C. Ehrenberg, *Repeat Buying, Facts, Theory and Applications,* 2nd ed. (New York: Oxford University Press, 1988).

2. A.S.C. Ehrenberg and G.L. Goodhardt, *Seventeen Essays on Understanding Buying Behavior* (New York: J. Walter Thompson Company, no date), chapters 6.2–6.3.

3. When Professor Ehrenberg read this chapter, he criticized on technical grounds my use of index numbers to analyze purchase frequency. He recommended the use of raw data. However, with a substantial number of brands to deal with, I was faced with the problem of comparing purchase frequency across product categories. Such comparisons are difficult because the average frequency differs between categories, so that brands must be compared with one another within their categories. I could see no alternative therefore but to use index numbers to describe each brand's purchase frequency compared to its category average. I believe that a brand with an index of 125 is in a similar position to a brand with the same index in another category, although the purchase frequency of the two brands may be different when measured in absolute terms.

4. In earlier chapters, I used figures for first-quarter 1991 market share, as well as the average for the second, third, and fourth quarters, to determine a brand's progress over the course of a year.

5. Ehrenberg, *Repeat Buying*, pp. 169–170.

6. It is possible that the difference in the degree of concentration of buying is a result of the Nielsen method of measuring sales in this research by purchase occasions and not by volume. I am not, however, persuaded that this hypothesis is valid.

7. Ehrenberg, *Repeat Buying*, pp. 42–45.

8. Ibid., p. 174.

9. Ibid., pp. 177–181.

10. John Philip Jones and Jan S. Slater, *What's in a Name? Advertising and the Concept of Brands*, 2nd ed. (Armonk, NY: M.E. Sharpe, 2003), pp. 136–162.

11. Ibid., pp. 67–69.

12

From Insight to Action

The key conclusions that emerge from this book are as follows:

- The STAS differential varies widely by brand. The strongest campaign can generate six times the amount of immediate sales as the weakest campaign.
- Seventy percent (projected) of campaigns have a positive immediate effect on sales, but in many cases this effect is small in the short term and nonexistent in the medium term. Sales of all brands are extremely volatile in the short term, so the effect of a positive STAS differential is often lost in the weeks when the brand is not advertised, thanks to pressures from competitive brands. As a result, the medium-term success rate of advertising is reduced to 46 percent (projected) of cases.
- The STAS differential is a gatekeeper. Only if a brand has a positive STAS differential will it have the opportunity to receive a number of further beneficial effects for the longer term. The most important of these is that a brand might become an established member of the homemaker's repertoire, with inbuilt repeat purchase; the level of repeat purchasing increases when the brand achieves a 10 percent market share.
- A positive STAS differential enables the sales of a brand to respond to a single advertising exposure in the purchase interval. This makes possible the release of funds that can be used to advertise the brand more continuously, to the longer-term advantage of the brand.

- The synergy generated by a positive STAS differential, working in cooperation with advertising intensity and low (promotional) pricing, boosts the sales-generating effect of advertising intensity (if it were working alone) by a factor of six. This synergy triples the effectiveness of low, promotional prices (if low price were to be the sole sales stimulus).
- Effective advertising influences—but not exclusively—a brand's internal momentum: the dynamic that represents the long-term effect of advertising. Effective advertising works in cooperation with a brand's functional excellence compared to its competitors, to encourage repeat purchase.

One of the major benefits of a brand's internal momentum is that consumers will accept a higher price—which means that the brand can rely less on consumer promotion, to the benefit of the brand's profitability.

The best-performing campaigns support even higher consumer prices. Price can increase with growing degrees of advertising intensity.

A positive STAS differential is a *necessary but not exclusive condition* for an advertising campaign to be successful in the medium term. Advertising intensity—media continuity—goes a long way to transforming a short-term effect into a medium-term one.

These points prompt certain types of action. In this chapter, I make specific recommendations, starting with the short term and ending with the extreme long term. I am addressing packaged goods companies and advertising agencies.

The Short-Term Effect of Advertising

1. The STAS differential should be a gatekeeper for your campaigns. If a brand achieves a positive STAS differential, you can safely make plans for prolonging the campaign's effect and turning a short-term into a medium-term success. But if the brand does not achieve a positive STAS differential, then you must immediately return to the drawing board.

2. The STAS data in this book are based on figures for the full year 1991. With large brands whose STAS is derived from large statistical subsamples, a STAS differential could probably be calculated from six months' data. It would be economic in the future for pure single-source systems to be set up in test markets. Remember that many successful

campaigns run for a number of years, and it is worth spending time and money in the first year to ensure that the campaign is generating a measurable sales effect that will, it is hoped, pay off over many years.

3. The STAS differential should be used as a diagnostic device for a brand that is experiencing a sales softening. Assuming that the problem does not stem from causes unconnected with the brand's advertising (e.g., the successful relaunch of a competitive brand), the STAS differential will tell whether there is an advertising problem caused by the creative content or by the budgetary and media elements of the campaign.

Creative Characteristics

4. The creative characteristics of successful campaigns are broadly definable (see Chapter 6). Use these characteristics to evaluate campaign ideas. They provide guideposts to judgment and a framework for communications research. These points are valuable tools for brand managers and other people responsible for advertising evaluation. They are less valuable as instructions for creative people, because they would then almost certainly lead to stereotyped creative solutions.

Advertising Budgets

5. In setting an advertising budget, advertisers should be conscious of the average share of voice for brands of different sizes in any category. Average advertising intensity is only one measure that should be used to fix an advertising budget, but it is one of the most important ones. Share of voice falls progressively as a brand increases in market share. With the use of a simple statistical table, it is easy to establish a basic advertising intensity, which can be fine-tuned by considering other marketplace factors relating to the brand. Table 12.1, which is intended to be simple to use, proposes specific budgetary levels for brands of different sizes. These budgetary levels are expressed as shares of voice.

6. Remember that the average shares of voice are calculated for a broad range of brands, most of which have stable market shares. For a brand to *increase* its market share, its advertising intensity should be higher than the levels set in Table 12.1.

7. It is important to determine what expenditure is necessary to ensure that most members of the target group are exposed to one advertisement in each period of advertising. Conventional notions of effective frequency—which support an average frequency level twice or three

Table 12.1

Average Advertising Intensity Ready-Reckoner

Share of market	Share of voice above (+) or below (−) share of market (percent)	Advertising intensity (share of voice per percent of market share)
1	+5	6.0
2	+5	3.5
3	+5	2.7
4	+4	2.0
5	+4	1.8
6	+4	1.7
7	+2	1.3
8	+2	1.2
9	+2	1.2
10	+4	1.4
11	+4	1.4
12	+4	1.3
13	+1	1.1
14	+1	1.1
15	+1	1.1
16	+2	1.1
17	+2	1.1
18	+2	1.1
19	=	1.0
20	=	1.0
21	=	1.0
22	−3	0.9
23	−3	0.9
24	−3	0.9
25	−5	0.8
26	−5	0.8
27	−5	0.8
28	−5	0.8
29	−5	0.8
30	−5	0.8

Source: John Philip Jones, "Ad Spending: Maintaining Market Share," *Harvard Business Review*, January–February 1990, 38–42.

times what is suggested here—produce considerable waste because of the onset of diminishing returns.

8. The advertising flights should be at a relatively low level of concentration, and if possible they should be run weekly. The objective should be that the target group should be exposed to a single advertisement within each flight, although many people will see more than this. If gaps in the schedule must be accepted for budgetary reasons, make them coincide with seasonal lows in category sales.

Advertising and Promotion

9. Do not advertise without some promotional support.

10. Do not promote without some advertising support.

11. The strategic planning of advertising and promotions should be integrated. Both activities should be timed to work in cooperation with each other, to maximize synergy. Creatively, advertising and promotions should communicate the same values as far as possible. This means that promotions should be used not only to generate sales but also for franchise-building. Promotions therefore need to be conceived with more regard to building added values than is common in the field of consumer goods today. In other words, promotional ideas call for a creative input.

12. For the most successful campaigns, tip the balance gradually toward more advertising and fewer promotions. This strategy should represent a long-term program to improve profitability and boost a brand's internal momentum.

Heavy Buyers

13. With every brand, part of the advertising and promotional effort should be directed at preserving the purchase frequency of the 20 percent of heaviest buyers. These people are likely to account for 60 percent of sales volume. This has creative, media, promotional, and packaging implications.

Internal Momentum

14. A brand's internal momentum represents its most permanent quality. A brand's longevity is a function of its internal momentum, which needs great effort to preserve and increase. This means care, attention, and the investment of time and money. The downward phase of the brand life cycle is almost always caused by a lack of these inputs, stemming either from deliberate neglect or lack of attention.

15. Important brands should never be put on the back burner. Success for a large brand is often measured by the maintenance (not necessarily increase) of its market share, and this also calls for care, attention, and investment. The profits that result from the scale economies of large brands are substantial enough to justify such continuous effort.

16. A brand should be improved to maintain its functional distinc-

tiveness, and such improvement should be part of a continuous program, including product testing the brand against its competitors.

17. Advertising campaigns should be refreshed regularly but should be consistent in the ways in which they project and nurture the brand's added values.

18. Every effort should be made to define the brand's added values. There are a number of projective research techniques that explain added values in multidimensional terms.

New Brands

19. Pure single-source research can be used as a diagnostic tool for new brand launches. The STAS analysis will reveal whether the advertising campaign is effective. An estimate of advertising intensity will disclose any problems with advertising continuity. An analysis of repeat-purchase rates will point to difficulties unrelated to advertising, such as functional inadequacies of the brand compared to its competitors, problems of price, or imperfections in retail distribution.

20. A brand's development should be monitored by the progress of its penetration and purchase frequency. Evaluate occasionally the frequency distribution of its purchases, its repeat buying rate, and its duplication with other brands. Changes in the patterns of duplication can point to dangerous and perhaps unexpected inroads by competitive brands.

21. Consumers' perceptions of the brand's image attributes should be measured continuously to ensure that the brand's added values are being preserved and augmented, not eroded. This tracking is a vital diagnostic tool.

22. As much effort should be devoted to evaluating competitive brands as to evaluating your own brands. This evaluation should encompass both the functional properties and the added values.

23. The STAS differential should be measured at intervals to check that the campaign still retains its competitive effectiveness.

24. An effort should be made to compute the price elasticity of every brand. This will help estimate the payoff of promotions in sales and profit. It will also guide you toward the optimum list price to maximize profitability.

25. One of the problems with research practice is its roots in the status quo. Dedicated to improvements and refinements within the limits set by the current situation, it does not encourage big leaps into an un-

known future. Manufacturers should encourage radically new types of research, despite the major costs and the uncertain rewards of such an endeavor. I am thinking about the exploration of what are, for marketing, untraditional fields, such as anthropology and symbiotics, which should be studied with the aim of generating hypotheses about the ways in which categories and brands might evolve, decades into the future. Such developments will inevitably be the responses to broad but gradual changes within society, and the marketing profession should be seeking to identify these changes. This is the most subtle and competitive way in which the internal momentum of brands can be gradually boosted.

III

Appendixes

——— Appendix A ———

Stability . . . and Volatility

In academic circles, marketing is sometimes spoken of as a scientific discipline. If it possesses such an unexpected intellectual respectability, a simple discovery dating from the early 1930s was what made it possible.

A scientific discipline is an activity with three special characteristics. It is based on an expanding body of accurate knowledge, it formulates and develops a doctrine derived from that knowledge, and the acolytes of the discipline have a mental attitude of objectivity and disinterestedness. Marketing was certainly not scientific until the discovery and widespread use of the A.C. Nielsen retail audit system, described in Appendix C.

A decade before World War II, this simple although expensive device transformed marketing guesswork into informed judgment based on a body of data. The Nielsen technique made it possible to evaluate with reasonable precision the competitive relationships between brands, the ebb and flow of seasonal sales movements, and a host of detailed sales patterns and distributional variations according to type of store and region of the country. Nielsen did this by providing reliable standardized data by category and by brand and variety, from two-month period to two-month period, year in and year out.

Above all, Nielsen was able to trace the long-term sales trends in product categories, market segments, and individual brands. The Nielsen retail audit led to much enlightenment, and its influence, although not 100 percent beneficial, was far more positive than negative.[1]

Smooth Sales Trends

Although the Nielsen system could measure many things, it was unable to detect short-term sales movements, for the obvious reason that the measurement cycle was relatively infrequent: stores were audited every two months. Nielsen was also inefficient at detecting advertising effects, except the very long-range ones. It did, however, generate crude but useful information on the results of promotions.

Nielsen data were presented in the form of simple charts covering extended periods, and they gave the overwhelming impression that sales movements are smooth and regular. The information had an apparently seamless quality, which carried a strong implication for the consumer behavior underlying the sales changes that were being monitored.

Figure A.1 plots the sales of the two leading brands in a major category of repeat-purchase packaged goods over five years, 1975 though 1979. In the first year, the two brands are approximately equal in size, but by the fifth year, XB had slipped about 15 percent behind XA. Over the period, XA dipped slightly and then recovered; XB showed gradual erosion in the fourth and fifth years. Sales changed direction only once for each brand, and then only slightly.

The inevitable impression made by this analysis—which is typical of the annual data produced by the Nielsen retail audit system—is that over the whole five-year period, the same large number of purchasers had continued buying brand XA with approximately the same purchase frequency. XB had also remained a substantial brand, although there had been some reduction in the number of its buyers and/or in the frequency of their buying it, beginning about halfway through the period. This gradual weakening was connected with a fall in the advertising investment in XB.[2] Although the line of reasoning here is logical, I want to make a different point: when we compare individual observations that follow each other, all the movements are relatively small.

Figure A.1 is a microcosm of the stability of the entire process of marketing consumer goods. Many of the leading American brands of the 1920s kept the same dominant position for decades and in many cases still retain this leadership today.[3] The large numbers of Nielsen retail audit analyses reported over the years reinforced the conclusion that market shares do not change much over time and that any changes that do take place are slow, although often progressive (which gives them a long-term impact). The overwhelming impression created by the Nielsen data was an absence of radical change.

Figure A.1   **Annual Sales of Brands XA and XB**
(index: sales of XA in 1975 = 100)

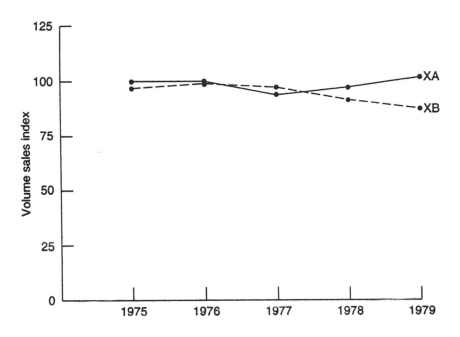

Since the Nielsen research system did not examine consumer behavior directly, only by inference, it was unable to examine some more subtle possibilities. When measured in consumer terms, a brand's sales in any period can be determined by a formula containing five elements, shown in Table A.1. (This table also appeared in Chapter 11 as Table 11.1.) Of these five elements, the two most important ones—those that distinguish one brand from another—are penetration (the number of houscholds that buy the brand at least once in a defined period) and purchase frequency (the average number of times they buy it). In different periods of equal length, the penetration and purchase frequency figures for any brand remain relatively constant. But as we examine shorter intervals, the amount of variation is seen to increase. For instance, a homemaker's buying may be concentrated into one small part of a year: in the first quarter there may be heavy purchases driven by promotions, and littly buying in the second, third, and fourth. When the annual figures are averaged, the result will be the same purchase frequency as in another year during which her purchases were more evenly distributed over the four quarters.

Table A.1

Sales and Consumer Behavior

Sales of a brand in a defined period = Household population
                       × Penetration
                       × Purchase frequency
                       × Packs bought per purchase occasion
                       × Average size of pack

Since most consumers have a repertoire of brands in each product category, a consumer may routinely change her patronage monthly or even weekly. In other words, her purchases dart about between brands, either erratically or (more probably) in response to specific marketing stimuli.

The longer the period over which we review a brand's sales, the more these variations will even out. The constancy of purchasing patterns does not end with penetration and purchase frequency. Year after year (when we compare annual figures), there are similarly unchanging patterns in the frequency distribution of consumer purchases, in consumers' repeat-buying patterns, and in their multibrand buying: the interconnected web of brands that constitute each homemaker's purchasing repertoire.[4] These long-term constants were examined in Chapter 11.

There is, however, a general principle covering all continuous tracking in the market place. The longer the period covered by each observation, the smaller and smoother the transition from number to number; and the shorter the period covered, the more erratic the movements from number to number.

One way of demonstrating this point is to look at Nielsen's bimonthly measures, which were the standard source of tactical market intelligence for more than half a century. Figures A.2 and A.3 examine approximately the last two years covered by Figure A.1, the period during which Brand XB began to decline. Figure A.2 shows bimonthly data for Brand XA; Figure A.3, for Brand XB. The obvious feature of these two diagrams is that these readings are more variable than the annual ones. But the variations follow a regular pattern, driven by seasonal trends. Both brands peak in the summer, and the dip from summer peak to winter trough is approximately 30 percent, about the same for both brands. It is also possible to see how XA is maintaining its overall sales level, while

Figure A.2   **Bimonthly Sales of Brand XA**
(index: sales in first period = 100)

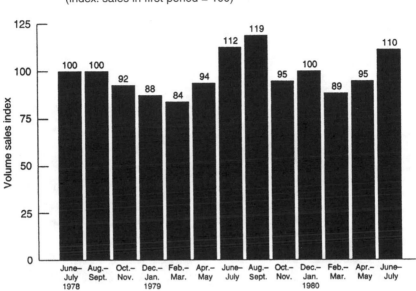

XB is trending downward slightly. Note that the figures reverse course only in response to seasonal movements. There is no erratic flickering back and forth. The seasonal sales movements are entirely predictable from the experience of previous years.

From this sort of analysis, it is rarely possible to demonstrate any short-term effect of advertising. With Brands XA and XB, there is no correlation between bimonthly advertising expenditure figures and bimonthly sales. But promotions are another story. We can draw some clear inferences, although the measurement tool is a clumsy one. To look at the effect of promotions, we must analyze Brand XA's share of market. Figure A.4 ignores the absolute changes in the size of the category, period by period; each column would total 100 percent if all brands were measured. By plotting shares exclusively, as in Figure A.4, we can exclude seasonal effects, which muddy the water because promotions take place in both high and low seasons.

Two conclusions stand out from Figure A.4. First, Brand XA's market share is moving upward to a modest degree. We saw in Figure A.1 that when measured in absolute terms XA's sales were only going up fractionally between 1977 and 1979. Its increased share in this period must therefore be a result of something else as well: a very slight de-

Figure A.3   **Bimonthly Sales of Brand XB**
(index: sales in first period = 100)

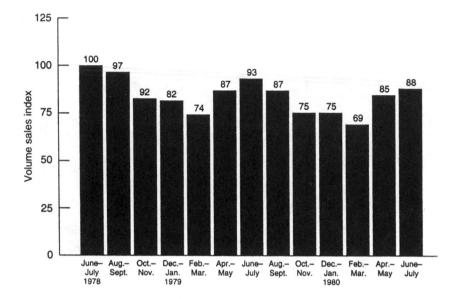

cline in the size of the category. This in fact is what happened in four of the two-monthly auditing periods covered in Figure A.4.

The second feature of Figure A.4 is a number of small, short-term ups and downs. The ups are associated with promotions: a loading of deal merchandise in the four months June through September 1979 and the combined effect of a number of specific deal activities, in particular special prices, during the four months December 1979 through March 1980. Note the sales dip—a return to normality—at the end of each promotional period. This standard pattern is described in the jargon used by the marketing people employed by Unilever as the *top hat effect*; the Nielsen chart, when it measures a promotional uplift over a single period, has a profile like a stovepipe hat.

There is not much finesse in how the Nielsen retail audit was able to measure the effect of promotions, but such an effect was certainly detectable in many cases. But as I have stated, advertising was not so measurable—a fact that had an unfortunate consequence.

Analysts became accustomed to finding so little relation between advertising and sales that some advertisers and agencies began to believe that there was no short-term effect to be measured. A doctrine was formulated, which in many quarters is believed to this day, that the sole

Figure A.4   **Bimonthly Market Share of Brand XA**

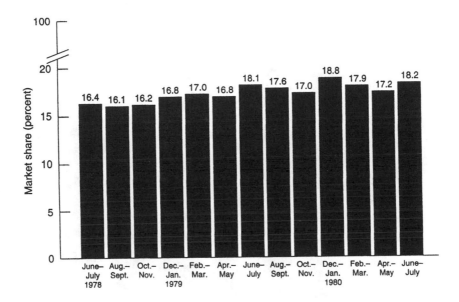

purpose of advertising is to strengthen the brand image, by reinforcing a brand's nonfunctional added values.[5] In other words, advertising provides only a long-term benefit, not a short-term one. Advertising often does have a long-term effect. But a doctrine focusing on long-term effects is seriously incomplete. This book is concerned with demonstrating that advertising is capable of stimulating sales strongly in the short term. What is more, unless there is a short-term effect, there will be no long-term one.

For lack of any demonstration of advertising's ability to sell goods immediately after its exposure, I believe that many advertisers during the 1980s and 1990s lost their faith in advertising as an engine to generate sales. This led to what I have termed "advertising's crisis of confidence": a major problem of perception that has caused stagnation in the advertising industry during recent years, both in the United States and abroad.[6]

The Arrival of Scanner Data

Scanner research produces its numbers every week. This information can be recomputed over bimonthly intervals, and in this way we can compare it to historical Nielsen retail audit data. Figures A.5 and A.6 are

Figure A.5 **Bimonthly Sales of Brand YA**
(index: based on sales in first week)

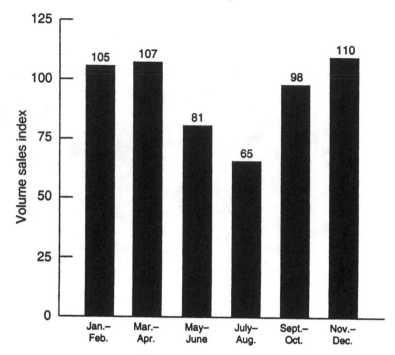

derived from scanner-based Nielsen research describing sales of brands
YA and ZA; these two diagrams are directly comparable to Figures A.2
(Brand XA) and A.3 (Brand XB).

The sales movements for Brands XA, XB, YA, and ZA are more similar
than dissimilar. All four brands have a pronounced seasonality, although
the dip from peak to trough is rather greater for YA and ZA than it is for
XA and XB. And YA and ZA peak in the winter; XA and XB, in the
summer. But the point I again want to emphasize is the predictability of
the transition from two-month period to two-month period. The only
reversals of course are the seasonal ones. All four examples reinforce
the impression that markets do not move erratically. There is a similar
regularity of patterns in them all.

If scanner data had been presented in bimonthly and not weekly intervals, our perceptions would remain today the same as they were before the 1980s. We would still believe that markets and brands do not
change much and that any changes are regular in the medium term and
gradual in the long term—an extraordinary misperception and oversim-

Figure A.6   **Bimonthly Sales of Brand ZA**
(index: based on sales in first week)

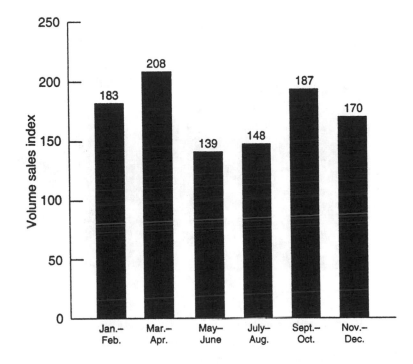

plification of the real world. Weekly data from scanner research make it abundantly clear that when we look at sales from an extremely short-term point of view, there is nothing short of ferment: rapid rises and falls and frequent changes of direction.

Examine the weekly data in Figure A.7 and compare them with the bimonthly data for the same brand in Figure A.5. Figure A.7 shows a typical pattern of extreme volatility. The sales level in every week is different from that in virtually every other, and some of the week-by-week swings are extremely pronounced. The drop from seasonal peak to trough is 62 percent, compared with the seasonal dip of 41 percent in the bimonthly figures in Figure A.5.

A similar picture emerges for Brand ZA in Figure A.8; compare this with the bimonthly figures in Figure A.6. Figure A.8, like Figure A.7, shows a restless to-and-fro movement from week to week. And the seasonal drop from peak to trough is again steep—60 percent—compared with the dip of 33 percent when the data are analyzed in bimonthly

Figure A.7   **Weekly Sales of Brand YA**
(index: sales in first week = 100)

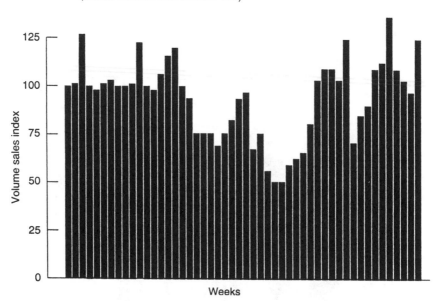

intervals. Both weekly diagrams show unpredictability in place of the regularity that was such a feature of the bimonthly charts.

The week-by-week variations in Figures A.7 and A.8 are typical of the hundreds of examples that scanner research has generated. They confirm and emphasize the truth of the general principle stated earlier in this chapter that the shorter the period covered by each observation, the more erratic the movements from number to number.

Of course, the important question we must now confront is this: What causes these erratic variations?

Part of the explanation must lie in promotions for the brand we are examining. (The examples of the evaluation of promotional effects that will be found in Appendix C were all derived from week-by-week analyses similar to those in Figures A.7 and A.8). We must also include the influence of promotions for competitive brands, which can cause immediate and temporary sales losses to our brand.

But promotions are not all. As I demonstrated in Chapter 2, advertising can also have a powerful short-term effect, evident from the short-term advertising strength (STAS) measure. And we must not forget the advertising for competitive brands, some of which will also have an

Figure A.8   **Weekly Sales of Brand ZA**
(index: sales in first week = 100)

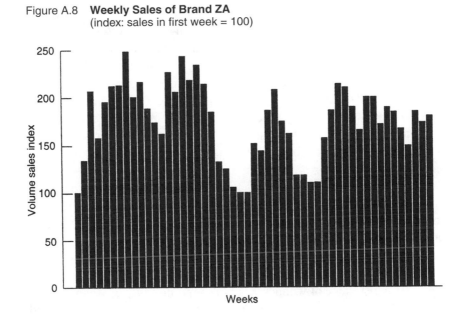

effective STAS, which may temporarily depress sales of our brand.

There is no doubt whatsoever that when measured weekly, the sales of most brands are volatile, and sometimes extremely so. But the movements are not erratic. They are in response to at least six forces, which do not operate haphazardly:

1. promotions for our brand
2. promotions for competitive brands
3. advertising for our brand
4. advertising for competitive brands
5. distributional problems (e.g., out of stock) for our brand
6. distributional problems for competitive brands

Forces 1, 3, and 6 cause sales of our brand to rise, and 2, 4, and 5 cause them to fall. In the background there are also some longer-term forces at work. Consumer satisfaction with the functional features of our brand will lubricate the short-term effect of advertising and promotions by encouraging repeat purchase. Consumer satisfaction with the functional features of competitive brands will reduce the effectiveness of our own advertising and promotions.

In the short term, sales of any brand constantly change direction. If there are more ups than downs, the brand is on a rising trend, but if there are more downs than ups, the trend is falling. If the ups and the downs balance, we see long-term stability. Markets are not smooth. Transitions are not seamless. But if there is an approximate balance in the forces driving a brand up and driving it down, the eventual result will appear to be smooth and unchanging. Nielsen retail audit figures oversimplified the movements and therefore misled us for years. Scanner research has provided the correction by looking deeper and in more detail at how sales actually move on an individual rather than a cumulative basis.

Nuclear physics provides an analogy, which I hope readers will not consider too fanciful. From the eighteenth to the twentieth centuries, scientists thought that matter, the substance from which the world is fashioned, was made up of collections of tiny solid particles that they called atoms. In the twentieth century, physicists found totally unexpected ways of examining atoms more and more closely. They saw, for the first time, a scene of wonder. Every atom is nothing less than a world in perpetual movement, and each piece of matter—in its complexity and dynamism—resembles a constantly changing universe.

Is the Volatility of Markets a New Discovery?

During the 1980s, a few analysts began to sense instinctively the subtle ways in which markets might be operating. The first release of scanner data provided confirmation and inspiration.

In 1984, Leo Bogart, then head of the Newspaper Advertising Bureau, examined a variety of data (including some based on scanner research) from five large packaged goods fields. He was surprised by what he found. "What appears to be a stable national market for packaged goods is actually extremely volatile. The volatility of purchase volume and brand share parallels what is found in studies of consumer behavior —a constant movement in buying plans and intentions, a constant switching of individual purchase preferences among brands."[7]

Bogart's paper draws many interesting conclusions. One of these has a bearing on a subject I have discussed in this book. When Bogart examined the effect of media exposure, he could trace only a limited sales response to advertising on television and in magazines. But the effect from newspapers was much more directly evident—an outcome he attributed to their promotional orientation: their call to direct action. On the other hand, the other media "work differently and with less immediate and universal impact. Their effects are usually spread through time, absorbed into the dense competitive communications environment, and untraceable, short run, at the point of sale."[8] Note the harmony between Bogart's conclusion about television and magazines and the theory described earlier in this chapter that advertising's effect is exclusively a long-term one.

I believe that there is a more plausible explanation for the apparently more evident effect from newspapers than from other media. The difference is caused by problems of measurement. In Appendix B, in my description of the McDonald study, I make the point that the advertising media were fewer and less complex in Great Britain in 1966 than they are in the United States today. In Britain, it was a relatively easy matter to track household exposure to the advertising for specific brands—in other words, to use the pure single-source method. I believe that this comparison of British and American media conditions holds the clue to an understanding of why Bogart found a greater advertising effect from newspapers than from television and magazines.

Bogart was basing his conclusion on data from a variety of sources. With media that contain as much advertising clutter as television and magazines, traditional research methods lack the precision to isolate the effect of the advertising campaigns for individual brands on the sales of those brands. The marginal effect of the specific campaign is lost in the aggregate effect of all the advertising in these dense and busy media.

But newspapers are a different story. Newspapers carry relatively little advertising for repeat-purchase packaged goods, and most areas of the country have only one or at most two newspaper titles. If we relate consumer purchases in any week to newspaper readership in the same week, there is very little aggregate advertising to confuse the relationship between brand advertising and brand purchase. If we know that a particular brand was advertised in a particular newspaper, we can reasonably assume that people were exposed to that brand's advertising when we measure household exposure to newspapers in general. In other words, we get quite close to the pure single-source research method.

Bogart's discovery of a strong advertising effect from newspapers was the result of his ability to get reasonably close to the crucial relationship of consumer exposure to advertising for a specific brand and purchase of that brand. The fact that Bogart found a positive short-term sales response from newspaper advertising is important. But with a better measurement tool, I believe that he would also have discovered a positive effect from the other media.

Bogart's conclusion about the underlying volatility of markets is echoed in the following comment, which was written at about the same time: "An individual's purchasing behavior may at first glance appear erratic and haphazard. But the more we study such behavior over time, and the more we look at the aggregate behavior of large numbers of consumers, the more regular and predictable it all appears to be."[9]

Notes

1. It certainly had one unintended consequence. It generated, or at least fueled, the theory of the product life cycle, one element of which is the dangerous and counterproductive notion that cyclical decline is inevitable. This is a myth that I have discussed in another place. John Philip Jones and Jan S. Slater, *What's in a Name? Advertising and the Concept of Brands*, 2nd ed. (Armonk, NY: M.E. Sharpe, 2003), pp. 52–54.

2. Ibid., pp. 88–89. In that context, XA is named Brand R, and XB is Brand Q.

3. See, for instance, "Old Standbys Hold Their Own," *Advertising Age*, September 19, 1983. Also see a list of the leading brands in 1923 and 2005, *Advertising Age*, March 14, 2005, p. 28.

4. Jones and Slater, *What's in a Name?* pp. 107–135.

5. A good example is Ogilvy's well-known observation: "The greater the similarity between brands, the less part reason plays in brand selection. The manufacturer who dedicates his advertising to building the most sharply defined *personality* for his brand will get the largest share of the market at the highest profit." David Ogilvy, *Confessions of an Advertising Man* (New York: Atheneum, 1984), p. 102.

6. John Philip Jones, "Advertising's Crisis of Confidence," *Marketing Management* 2, no. 2 (1993), pp. 14–24.

7. Leo Bogart, *The Turbulent Depths of Marketing: An Analysis of Supermarket Scanner Data* (New York: Newspaper Advertising Bureau, 1984), p. 14. I presented some of my own tentative findings from the Nielsen single-source database to a meeting of the Market Research Council in New York City in March 1993. Dr. Bogart was present at this meeting and was interested in my conclusions regarding the apparent stability yet underlying volatility of markets. He subsequently sent me a copy of his own 1984 paper, which had been distributed fairly widely although I had not seen it before. I subsequently published it. See Leo Bogart, "The Turbulent Depths of Marketing," in *How Advertising Works: The Role of Research*, ed. John Philip Jones, pp. 26–48. (Thousand Oaks, CA: Sage Publications, 1998).

8. Bogart, "The Turbulent Depths of Marketing" in *How Advertising Works*, p. 47

9. Jones and Slater, *What's in a Name?* p. 109.

Appendix B

The History of Single-Source Research
The First Steps

The pioneer work in single-source research was carried out in Great Britain in 1966. It has become known as the McDonald study, taking its name from Colin McDonald, the man most responsible for it. Two researchers were in fact involved in planning this investigation: Timothy Joyce and McDonald, and it is worth saying a few words about them.

Joyce and McDonald are good examples of the versatile generalists who sometimes emerge from the most traditional type of British education. Both men were educated in the humanities: Joyce in moral sciences (i.e., philosophy) and McDonald in "Greats" (i.e., the Greek and Latin classics and philosophy). These are often thought to be effective disciplines to develop a student's analytical powers, an assumption that is not always ill-founded.

Both Joyce and McDonald began their careers in market research during the 1950s, and it did not take them long to master the technical aspects of the business. But their nonspecialist liberal education helped them to look at market research problems in an open, innovative way, and their mental discipline helped them focus continuously on the essentials of each problem until they had found a solution to it. These qualities are what gave birth to the concept of single-source research.

During the 1960s, Joyce and McDonald were both working at the British Market Research Bureau (BMRB), the research company owned by the J. Walter Thompson (JWT) advertising agency. BMRB had been for decades one of the largest and most successful research organizations in the United Kingdom. Although operating independently from JWT, the two organizations have many clients in common.

The challenge that Joyce and McDonald faced was a matter of major continuous importance to an agency like JWT: what is the effect of advertising? Most agencies have speculated about this question for decades, and some of them have spent much money trying to find answers. When Joyce and McDonald (among others) were given the problem, they began by narrowing down the question into something that could be tackled within the technical limits of market research as it was practiced during the 1960s, at the same time keeping within the budget provided by JWT to cover the cost of the project. They therefore decided to concentrate exclusively on advertising's short-term effect. A number of findings of operational value emerged from their research, findings that were used on a proprietary basis by JWT on behalf of its clients. This is the reason there was a delay of five years between the original fieldwork and analysis, and McDonald's first publication of the findings.[1]

How McDonald's Research Was Conducted

The tool used for the research was the household diary. In 1966 this was a well-established device widely and productively employed in both the United States and Great Britain. In the 1960s, the only method of collecting diary data was by using pencil and paper: The homemaker was required to fill in a diary of her day-to-day purchases. What made the McDonald research unusual was that each respondent was also asked to fill in details of her media exposure—the viewing times of the television programs and commercial breaks she had viewed and the issues she had seen from a list of thirty-two newspapers and magazines.[2] In 1966, there was only one British television channel running advertising, so it was a simple matter for the tabulators to log the actual brands that appeared on air during the commercial breaks each homemaker had viewed. It was also fairly easy to list the brands advertised in the various issues of the thirty-two newspapers and magazines she claimed to have seen.

When McDonald measured advertising exposure, he did not assume that everyone looking at a particular commercial break or at a specific newspaper or magazine actually saw all the advertising in those media. McDonald used the concept, common in Britain, of potential exposure to advertising, or opportunity-to-see (OTS). McDonald measured the number of a brand's OTS immediately before purchase, and this is the number he related to the buying of the brand.

The diary method made it possible to put together *within each household* the brands purchased by the homemaker at any time and the advertising for those same brands that she was exposed to just before she did her buying. In this way the framework for the first single-source research project was established. (The breakdown into individual households is called disaggregation.)

For reasons of cost and practicability, the investigation was confined to a single geographical area, London, and to a thirteen-week period. The total sample of households was 255. Nine categories of repeat-purchase packaged goods were covered: bread, breakfast cereals, margarine, milk drinks, shampoo, soup, tea, toothpaste, and washing powder. These varied in their advertising intensity.[3]

The problematical aspects of the research plan were, first, that the method of data collection was relatively primitive (by the standards of later years), and second, that the scale of the operation was small. The plan of the investigation was nevertheless clean and focused, the whole project was carried through efficiently, and it was subsequently described by McDonald in an impeccable paper.

The greatest innovation of the research was the bringing together, respondent by respondent, of advertising exposure and brand purchasing. This seems in retrospect an obvious way of tackling the question that the research was designed to answer. It was, nevertheless, a tactic that had never been followed before. I suspect that the research industry had never moved along the path taken by McDonald because the business was developing in precisely the opposite direction: toward larger size and an increasing aggregation of research data. This made McDonald's move toward disaggregation a startling reversal of the trend.

As discussed in Chapter 1, none of the single-source research carried out in the United States or anywhere else during the 1980s managed to disaggregate the really important data right down to the individual household. None of it could simultaneously collect the information on advertising exposure for a brand before purchase and on the actual buying of that brand. This is the system described in Chapter 1 as pure single-source: the method at the heart of the Nielsen single-source research on which this book is based.

McDonald's use of the purchase interval is also worth mentioning. Since it encompasses the time between the buyer's last purchase of a brand in the category and her next one, it provides the most precise possible definition of the period during which the short-term effect of advertising should be measured. It also allows for differences between categories and brands, since their purchase intervals differ.

McDonald calculated the influence of advertising on purchase by counting buyers who had changed their brand after having been exposed to advertising for it during the interval since the preceding purchase. He also counted the number of people staying with their previously purchased brand after having been exposed (similarly) to its advertising. The main conclusions of the research, however, were based on brand switching.

Switching, often called brand rotation, is normal in virtually all categories of repeat-purchase packaged goods, because most consumers have a repertoire of brands they buy with different approximate degrees of regularity. Even if some consumers have not received advertising for a brand, they are likely to rotate their buying to it anyway. But McDonald's precise juxtaposition of the advertising prompt and the subsequent purchase enabled him to measure the extra effect of the advertising in isolation.

When viewed over the medium term (normally a period between three and twelve months), a brand's penetration (i.e., user base) tends to remain constant because the number of people rotating into a brand tends to balance the number rotating out.[4] This balance tends to keep the brand's market share more or less constant. McDonald's technique measured the extent to which advertising succeeded in generating a net increase in switching into the brand. However, McDonald did not claim that this was a permanent effect; the process of rotation continues after the upward blip stimulated by the advertising. The increase in market share is therefore only temporary.

One problem caused by the use of brand switching was that certain buyers had to be excluded from the tabulations. These were sole buyers (i.e., buyers of only one brand in the category), nonbuyers of the brand being examined, and people unexposed to advertising in the field.[5] These omissions, although necessary, reduced the size of an already small sample.

In my own work with Nielsen data, I have followed McDonald's procedure of relating the respondent's exposure to advertising for the brand to her purchase of it. I have, in other words, recreated McDonald's pure

Table B.1

Comparison of McDonald's and Jones's Single-Source Studies

	McDonald	Jones	Approximate multiplication factor
Sample size	255	2,000	× 8
Test span	13 weeks	52 weeks	× 4
Number of categories	9	12	× 1.3
Total			× 42

single-source method. There are, however, two differences between McDonald's system of measurement and mine, both related to the much larger scale of my own research (see Table B.1). This has caused problems of tabulation because of the complexity of the computer programs Nielsen had to employ.

First (as explained in Chapter 1), I have standardized the purchase interval during which the advertising is measured to the seven days preceding purchase. Second, I do not use brand switching as my means of measuring advertising's effect. Instead, I use short-term advertising strength (STAS), a measure derived from market share. My preference for this device stems partly from its much greater simplicity and partly because it is the method I used most often during my professional career. I was always taught to examine advertising's effect by looking for changes in a brand's share of market (SOM). This book is devoted virtually exclusively to SOM, because I have been searching for *differences in advertising effectiveness between brands.* In this respect my investigation covers different ground from McDonald's. He was most concerned with advertising's average effect across brands. He was not concerned with individual brand variations, although in one of McDonald's earlier papers he presented a narrow range of evidence that advertising effects can vary significantly between brands, at least within one product category he managed to explore. This is a tantalizing digression that McDonald was unable to develop because of the limitations imposed by his sample size.[6]

McDonald's Main Conclusions

McDonald was concerned essentially with examining advertising's short-run effect, as demonstrated by data that he averaged. His most impor-

Table B.2

Effect on Brand Switching of Two Basic Levels of Advertising Exposure

	Percent of switches to advertised brand after 0 or 1 OTS	Percent of switches to advertised brand after 2 or more OTS
Bread	50.2	56.3
Breakfast cereal	49.8	51.3
Margarine	49.9	51.0
Milk drinks	53.7	55.9
Shampoo	47.6	50.0
Soup	49.4	52.2
Tea	48.1	62.8
Toothpaste	47.4	54.7
Washing powder (laundry detergent)	49.6	52.4
Unweighted average for all categories	49.5	54.1

tant finding, by far, is that advertising can be demonstrated to have such an effect: an effect that operates consistently over all nine product fields covered in the research. The point was made in three separate ways, but was demonstrated with greatest precision in an analysis of switches to the advertising brand. These data are presented in Table B.2. This table is more complex than it looks, but can be explained by the following four points.[7]

- The table covers brand switches, or occasions in which a change of brand takes place between purchases.
- It percentages the switches to the advertised brand out of the total of all switches into and out of the same advertised brand. Each brand is counted in turn. (This is a very laborious procedure, but it was done because McDonald was searching for the purest possible measure of advertising effect.)
- The two columns compare the effect on brand switching of different quantities of advertising received by respondents.
- Each percentage is an average for all advertised brands in its category.

The higher numbers in the second column show clearly that something happened as a consequence of the larger amount of advertising: this had triggered a consistently higher proportion of brand switching. On average, across all nine categories, the proportion of switches stimulated by two or more OTS was 4.6 percentage points higher than the proportion that followed zero or one OTS. This increase represents a boost of 9 percent (4.6 percentaged on 49.5).

It may strike readers as peculiar that all the figures in Table B.2 are close to 50. The market shares of the brands that were averaged in each product category surely varied much more than this. McDonald's data are the direct product of his research method. Since switching into the brand is matched—within each consumer's purchasing—by her switching out of another brand, 50 percent would be the expected level if advertising had no effect. This explains also why there is a negative response from one advertising exposure. As McDonald notes, "The point is again the balance between $0 \rightarrow X$ (switching into the brand) and $X \rightarrow 0$ (switching out of the brand) within each individual. If this is equal, then overall the total, $0 \rightarrow X$ plus $X \rightarrow 0$, across all advertising levels must give a 50 : 50 result. So if 2+ OTS pushes the $0 \rightarrow X$ percentage above 50, then the other side, 0/1 OTS must balance by being below 50."[8]

The data in Table B.2 provide one of the classic pieces of aggregated evidence that advertising produces a short-term effect. I am, however, convinced that if McDonald had been working with a statistical sample large enough to break down the category figures, and in particular if he had analyzed advertising response by brand, his results would have shown large variability. For certain brands the response would have been shown to be much greater (and perhaps more immediate) than the averages, and with other brands there would have been no response whatsoever. In the few cases in which McDonald was able to pull out individual brand data, the variations confirm my conclusion that he was in general forced to aggregate his figures by product category. This meant that very important variations between brands were flattened, which effectively masked important truths. These variations are discussed in Chapter 2 of this book.

Returning to McDonald's main conclusions, the data on continuity of purchase show a similar increase to that shown in Table B.2. These figures demonstrate that advertising at a level of at least two OTS before purchase produces higher amounts of repeat purchase than zero advertising or only one OTS.[9]

McDonald showed that the greatest effect of advertising takes place four, three, or two days before purchase.[10] (This influenced my original decision to concentrate my own study on advertising received shortly before purchase, using a window of seven days before.) McDonald also

Table B.3

Effect on Brand Switching of Small Increments of Advertising Exposure

	Percent of switches to advertised brand in all categories
After zero OTS	50.1
After 1 OTS	46.8
After 2 OTS	54.0
After 3 OTS	53.3
After 4 or more OTS	53.7

found directional evidence that exposure levels of advertising in print media have a similar effect to those of commercials on television. However, since relatively little advertising for repeat-purchase packaged goods appears in print media, the database for examining the response to print advertising is thin.[11]

One or Two Advertising Exposures?

One of the most striking findings of McDonald's research relates to the differential effects of different levels of advertising exposure. The reader has seen in Table B.2 that the exposure data by product category are aggregated into two large groups—brand switches preceded by zero or one OTS, and switches preceded by two or more OTS. If we wish to break these groups down into smaller packets, into individual increments of advertising—zero, one, two, three, four, or more OTS—the subsamples per category are going to become unacceptably small. However, if we total up all nine categories, the advertising exposure data can then be broken down into individual OTS. This is done in Table B.3.[12] The rather startling conclusions from Table B.3 are that one OTS has less effect than zero and that the sales effect peaks at two OTS and thereafter shows no improvement from further advertising.

The findings of Table B.3 had a considerable influence on the advertising industry's concept of media strategy. Before the publication of McDonald's work in the United States, the notion of effective frequency had grown out of the work of analysts such as Herbert E. Krugman, Robert C. Grass, and Hubert A. Zielske, who had all been concerned with cognitive effects, not related to purchasing. A doctrine was gradually developed that significantly influenced advertising practice. The underlying theory was most persuasively expressed by Krugman when he hypothesized that three exposures of an advertisement are necessary to generate action:

1. The first, to prompt the respondent to try to understand the nature of the stimulus; and the respondent asks the question, "What is it?"
2. The second, to stimulate evaluation ("What of it?") and recognition ("I've seen this before").
3. The third, to remind (and also the beginning of disengagement).[13]

McDonald's work provided an empirical underpinning and strengthening of the doctrine that one advertising exposure is too weak to get through to the consumer.

The explanations by Krugman and the other psychological researchers of why one exposure is not enough are more complicated (and I believe less persuasive) than McDonald's own entirely lucid explanation, which is rooted in common sense. To McDonald, a brand needs two strikes to counteract the advertising of competitive brands. If a number of brands run advertising that is seen by the consumer in the interval before purchase, a brand with two OTS will win over a brand with only one: "It does not mean that one advertising exposure has no effect. It does suggest, however, that as far as short-term stimulating effect is concerned, one exposure tends to be beaten by two or more occurring at the same time, and this could have implications for scheduling tactics."[14] (This is an understatement of what actually happens.) Note in particular McDonald's admission that advertising is capable of having an effect from only one exposure. This is an important point that is underscored by my own research.

In my judgment, the psychological theories are persuasive when explaining the effect on viewers of new campaigns. But for existing and established campaigns, the first two stages—understanding and evaluation—have already taken place. After it has become part of the scenery, repeated exposures in effect represent reprises of the third stage—the reminding stage—of the communication process. Each advertisement now provides a stimulus for the consumer to buy the brand when she is next in the store. This is my reason for believing that the effectiveness of a single advertising exposure can be explained in terms of the psychological theories, and it is why the data in this book do not refute these theories.

There is no doubt that the psychological theories (which I think were misunderstood) and McDonald's research (which misled because it did not look at individual brands) led the advertising industry in a wrong direction. A hypothesis developed into a concept, which spawned a doctrine, which was transformed into a mantra.

Beginning in the 1960s, advertising agencies, media analysts, and trade press journalists produced an unending flow of argument and recommendations concerning the amount of advertising frequency necessary to affect sales.[15] One result of all this activity is that standard media planning practice in most American advertising agencies began (or continued with greater emphasis) to employ flights, or concentrations of gross rating points dense and heavy enough to ensure that the average viewer receives two OTS (or more commonly three for safety). Television viewing is distributed in such a way that to aim for two or three OTS means that a substantial minority of viewers will receive a much greater weight of advertising than this.

A media policy of this type has unexpected consequences. It is capable of generating great waste. As discussed in Chapter 5, there is evidence that a good deal of advertising works according to a pattern of diminishing returns, that is, with reducing marginal effectiveness as its quantity is increased. In many cases this pattern begins at the first exposure.[16] If a general policy of media concentration results in many advertisers packing their advertising into high-density bursts, it is likely that the extra frequency above the absolute minimum thought necessary for an effect will be operating with very real diminishing returns—in other words, uneconomically.

I believe that the effective frequency doctrine, to which McDonald's research added much reinforcement, contributed to a counterproductive and wasteful use of advertising money. McDonald himself is not to be blamed; he described his research from the beginning as nothing more than a small-scale experiment that should be treated with caution.

A massive, multitiered edifice was built on top of the very small foundation constructed by the psychological theorists and by McDonald. One of the purposes of this book is to use additional research to test whether this foundation is able to support everything that has been built on top of it. In particular, I have examined the circumstances when sales may respond to a single advertising exposure. If and when any campaign stimulates such a response, the media budget would be spent most economically by being deployed with minimal concentration and maximum dispersion. In the United States such a doctrine was initially regarded as unorthodox and perhaps heretical.

One of the main findings from the research to which this book is devoted is that advertising effects vary a great deal between brands. This suggests the strong possibility that some advertising campaigns need two strikes to have an effect, but some may not. For such brands, media dispersion would certainly be the better strategy. Five years after the publication of the first edition of this book, industry practice began to change radically as this lesson began to sink in (see Chapter 5).

Notes

1. McDonald's report was published at different times by the Market Research Society (MRS), the European Society for Opinion and Marketing Research (ESOMAR), and the Marketing Science Institute (MSI). Most recently and authoritatively, the paper occupied a prominent part of a book published by the Association of National Advertisers (ANA). The references in these endnotes will be to this source. Colin McDonald, "What Is the Short-Term Effect of Advertising?" in *Effective Frequency: The Relationship Between Frequency and Advertising Effectiveness,* ed. Michael J. Naples, (New York: Association of National Advertisers, 1979), pp. 83–103.

2. Ibid., p. 84.

3. Ibid.

4. John Philip Jones and Jan S. Slater, *What's in a Name? Advertising and the Concept of Brands,* 2nd ed. (Armonk, NY: M.E. Sharpe, 2003), pp. 116–117.

5. McDonald, "What Is the Short-Term Effect of Advertising?" p. 90.

6. Colin McDonald, "Relationships Between Advertising Exposure and Purchasing Behavior," *Journal of the Market Research Society,* 1970, pp. 89–91.

7. McDonald, "What Is the Short-Term Effect of Advertising?" p. 95.

8. Colin McDonald, personal communication, September 28, 1993.

9. McDonald, "What Is the Short-Term Effect of Advertising?" p. 94.

10. Ibid., pp. 100–101.

11. Ibid., p. 99.

12. Ibid., p. 96.

13. See Krugman's three articles, "The Measurement of Advertising Involvement," *Public Opinion Quarterly,* Winter 1966–67, pp. 583–596; "Why Three Exposures May Be Enough," *Journal of Advertising Research,* December 1972, pp. 11–14; and "What Makes Advertising Effective?" *Harvard Business Review,* March–April 1975, pp. 96–103.

14. McDonald, "What Is the Short-Term Effect of Advertising?" p. 97.

15. One of the major contributions to this development was the book edited by Naples, the details of which are given in note 1. It is also true that this book was published in response to the large amount of interest in the effective frequency concept within the advertising industry.

16. Jones and Slater, *What's in a Name?* pp. 177–181.

——— Appendix C ———

The History of Single-Source Research
Chasing Hares

The most important technical innovation to influence single-source research—and in effect to lift it off the ground—was the Universal Product Code (UPC). This strip of numbers and precisely printed lines of various thicknesses is an unobtrusive device that can be seen on virtually all packages of consumer goods. It holds exact information that can be read when put in contact with an electronic scanner, a seemingly uncomplicated apparatus that nevertheless employs a laser and a miniature computer. The scanner can either be a fixture on a store's checkout counter or handheld. The scanner reads the UPC and instantaneously records the main details of the package—manufacturer, brand name, variety, and size.

The UPC was developed to increase the efficiency of retailing: to speed the customer through the checkout. Prices are added by the retailer's own computer. Scanners began to come into general use in the mid-1970s, and within a few years they had become the predominant method of ringing sales at cash registers. They are used today for all types of repeat-purchase packaged goods and most other sorts of products as well.[1]

It did not take long for market researchers to sense the potential of the scanner for collecting research data, particularly for tracking sales on a continuous basis. The two most common research methods for measuring sales to consumers are to count them through the retail store and to measure them as they enter the household as consumer purchases. These two types of information may appear to be the same. But the main emphasis of the first type is on brands, segments, and categories, in other words, information seen from the manufacturer's point of view. The main point about the second type is that it is concerned with the characteristics of consumers: both their demography and their purchasing patterns.

Before scanners came into use, consumer sales out of the retail store were audited by the method invented by William B. Murphy and introduced by A.C. Nielsen Sr. during the early 1930s. This method was simple but laborious. A panel of stores was signed up, and the Nielsen researchers would regularly call on each. In order to calculate consumer sales during a defined period (Nielsen worked with two-month intervals), the researchers counted (A) the inventories of a brand within the store at the beginning of the period, (B) deliveries of the brand into the store during the course of the period, and (C) inventories at the end. It was then a simple matter to add A and B and deduct C, to calculate the *disappearance*—which meant essentially the units that had been sold to the consumer—during the interval.

The traditional method of collecting individual data on consumer purchases was to sign up a relatively stable panel of consumers, each of whom would use the pencil-and-paper home-diary method, described in the discussion of the McDonald study in Appendix B.

The UPC code and the scanner now offered something very much better. Retail sales could be tracked in full detail—a single purchase occasion at a time—from the information collected at the store checkout. By the early 1990s, the new research system had become securely established in the food trade, although the old audit system has only recently been abandoned in drug stores and mass merchandisers. The scanner system, being much simpler than the Nielsen audit method, brought cost advantages by reducing the traditionally very high expense of retail audit fieldwork.

But in addition to the cost saving, sales could now be measured more often. This represented a very major advantage as far as the supply of data was concerned. Weekly figures are now the norm, and there is no substantive reason that data collection should not even be done daily. The increase in the amount of data generated has been exponential, leading to a constant stream of complaints from both research practitioners and their clients about the sheer quantity of information generated. Many market research departments in manufacturing organizations have had to be reorganized to deal with it.

Measurement of consumer purchases with scanners also provides a plentiful source of data on consumers' demography and brand-buying habits. But there was an initial glitch in this part of the system. For many years, consumer purchases had to be logged in the store, because handheld scanners were not at first available. Each consumer on the panel was asked to use a plastic card when she passed through the checkout, making it possible to keep a record of all the details of her purchases. But the plastic cards were only accepted by some of the stores in the consumer's neighborhood, which meant that there were gaps in the data collection. There was also a problem of forgetfulness: shoppers not presenting their cards and cashiers not asking for them at the checkout. This card is sometimes known as a passive system. It is, perhaps, overpassive.

Filling out diaries on paper did at least have the advantage of recording information about all the homemaker's purchases no matter where they had been made. But paper-and-pencil data collection depended on consumers taking the trouble to list accurately all the goods they had bought. This difficulty was eventually solved by the introduction of the handheld scanner. Each panel member could now be equipped with a scanner for use at home to pick up the UPC information from all her purchases. All the Nielsen data on consumer purchasing described in this book were collected in this way.

It is not an exaggeration to say that during the 1980s, the entire business of sales research was transformed by the scanner. Some syndicated scanner services came and went. But two substantial organizations remain, operating in intense competition with each other: Information Resources Inc. (IRI) and A.C. Nielsen. The main retail measurement service run by IRI is called InfoScan; Nielsen has ScanTrack.

The consumer panel research run by IRI comprises a national panel and a test panel called BehaviorScan. This covers eight regions and operates with controlled television exposure: each home in the panel receives identified cable channels, and IRI's clients can vary the advertising weight and/or the copy in each region. The system is therefore geared to market experimentation. In contrast, the Nielsen Household Panel is fully national.

For single-source research, we must of course focus on the consumer

Table C.1

Types of Research Data Provided by Different Sales Tracking Techniques

Retail sales research	Consumer panel research
Consumer sales	Consumer purchasing
Trade promotions	Penetration
Consumer promotions	Purchase frequency
Pricing	Purchase frequency distribution
Distribution	Multibrand purchasing
Display	Repeat purchase
Competitive brand activity	Consumer promotions
	Consumer demographics
	General advertising exposure (from diluted single-source research)
	Specific advertising exposure (from pure single-source research)

panels. These are reasonably efficient in collecting data, barring the problem of the data gaps when handheld scanners are not used. Nielsen employs them, but IRI still relies on scanners at the store checkout. Despite this imperfection, there is some advantage to the IRI system. It makes it possible to collect a wealth of information specifically related to the retail store, particularly the details of competition between brands. The Nielsen ScanTrack panel of 3,000 stores provides comparable data to the IRI panel. ScanTrack and the Nielsen Household Panel are run as separate operations.

Aside from the potential gaps in the collection of the sales data, the most substantial imperfections of all the consumer panels are that they are mostly confined to small local areas and that there have been problems with the measurement of the media that come into the household. Specifically, none of the systems was able to get to the heart of media measurement by employing what I have described in this book as the pure single-source technique. This was, at least, the situation until the full Nielsen Household Panel service came into operation.[2]

Before looking at some of the uses to which scanner research has been put, it would be useful to itemize the various types of information that retail sales research and consumer panel research can provide (see Table C.1). This is a very rich range of possibilities. It offers so many attractive options that the market research industry has spent much time pursuing alluring (and sometimes inconsequential) alternatives. This is why I have entitled this appendix "Chasing Hares." To change the metaphor, there were so many goods in the market research store competing for attention during the 1970s and 1980s that the industry lost its focus or at least its interest in advertising effects.

In its early days, scanner research was used most energetically for a purpose that answered a very practical need. But regrettably this involved the first dilution of the single-source concept. The technique was directed at the problem of determining the optimum weight and frequency patterns of television advertising schedules. Scanner research in effect was moved into agency media departments.

Chasing the First Hare: Media Research

Appendix B describes how the concept of effective frequency received a new impetus as a result of the McDonald study. Scanner research made an important additional contribution by enabling planners to evaluate accurately the actual opportunities-to-see achieved for specific user groups. For many years—until at least 1986—this fascinating research device was focused more intently on media planning, buying, and evaluation than on any other marketing problem.[3]

A good way of reviewing the progress of scanner research is to look at the activities of the Advertising Research Foundation (ARF), as recorded in its various publications. The ARF was in the vanguard of the study of effective frequency and was the driving force behind the book that opened up McDonald's work to a wide audience in 1979.[4] This book, which caused much stir, was followed in 1982 by a major conference devoted to effective frequency, at which McDonald participated in 1982.[5]

During the 1980s, the ARF began to sponsor conferences in New York specifically concerned with scanner research. In the period 1988 through 1991 alone, five conferences were held that together produced eighty-one papers presented by researchers, advertisers, and advertising agency people.[6] The standard of these papers was understandably variable, but the best of them are even today extremely interesting. Nevertheless, the most striking—and disturbing—feature of the papers is that none of them present data derived from pure single-source research as defined in this book. All the research presented is based on diluted methods.

As a matter of minor interest, the phrase *single-source* was first used in the mid-1960s in the United Kingdom, apparently coined by the late

Table C.2

Brand Leverage Indexes, Primetime Network Programs: Third-Quarter, 1984

Program	Nielsen household rating	Brand A	Brand B	Brand C
St. Elsewhere	12.6	127	114	86
Cheers	16.8	122	114	95
Hill Saint Blues	16.9	115	124	87
Dallas	24.6	103	100	113
Ripley	12.8	95	124	84
The Jeffersons	15.7	93	89	124

Simon Broadbent, of the Leo Burnett advertising agency. In the United States, the phrase was first employed in 1979.[7]

The eighty-one ARF papers presented between 1988 and 1991 contained much discussion of the media applications of single-source research. Thirty-two papers were based on case studies of different types, and a number of these had a media focus. These demonstrated that the three main suppliers of consumer-based scanner research, IRI and Nielsen, plus SAMI-Arbitron (no longer in business), all offered ways of securing the best match between patterns of brand buying and television viewing.[8] The advertisers and agencies commissioning the research obviously wanted to use it to achieve the most cost-efficient media coverage of the users of specific brands.

Which Media? Which Programs?

Tools have been developed to compare the relative value of alternative media (e.g., television and magazines) for different brands. These methods help us to arrive at the best split of advertising budget between these media, and this division is likely to be different for each brand.[9]

At a more detailed level, finely tuned information can be provided about the coverage of media vehicles, in particular specific television programs. Table C.2 provides an example. The information in this table, presented by Roger Godbeer of Colgate-Palmolive, compares a number of television programs according to their brand leverage index: index numbers calculated from estimates of how many users of specific brands watched each show. The basic data were provided by IRI's BehaviorScan.[10] Table C.2 contains data of very practical value to media planners.

St. Elsewhere is the lowest rated of all six shows analyzed, yet it provides the best coverage of users of Brand A. *Dallas* is the top-rated show, yet it offers above-average coverage only of users of Brand C.

Such permutations of detailed media information are unquestionably valuable for weighing a brand's budget between media vehicles, on the basis of how well they get to its users. And similar data can be used for working out the most efficient regional variations, to improve an advertiser's tactics in the complicated market place for spot television.

Knowledge like this—if it were widely used—has the potential to increase the efficiency of media buying. However, media planning is carried out in a stereotyped, conservative way in many agencies, probably because historical data are regarded as poor predictors of future ratings. The excellent data provided by diluted single-source research are often neglected, and even this information only scratches the surface of what single-source research can provide. And it also introduces a serious problem with priorities.

By concentrating so much scanner research on routine matters like assessing program coverage to improve the cost-efficiency of media buying, single-source researchers were effectively diverted from a much more important task. This is to ensure that the strategy on which the buying plan is based is itself well founded.

McDonald's original research employed the pure single-source method, but only in a small-scale pilot investigation carried out in a foreign country more than two decades ago. In the United States, McDonald's tentative conclusion was used to support a number of pieces of theoretical, hardly robust psychological analysis. What had started as a hypothesis soon became widely accepted as the effective frequency doctrine, which became embodied in the media strategy for a huge number of advertised brands. Since the underlying strategic premise was no longer disputed, the advertising industry employed diluted single-source research simply to ensure that this strategy was executed as efficiently as possible.

This approach tackles a minor problem before a major one. I believe it would be more useful for the advertising industry to use single-source research to evaluate—to confirm or deny—the validity of the underlying strategy of effective frequency for specific brands. To do this, the sales effects of advertising must be measured case by case. This type of measurement was long neglected because attention was devoted instead to the interesting and modestly useful media applications that occupied so much of the energy and resources of single-source researchers.

When, in 1979, the ARF made a serious proposal to test McDonald's study by conducting a similar piece of research in the United States, the project was abandoned.[11] The research industry was too occupied in chasing a hare. The cleverest people were too busy using their ingenuity to build the most efficient television schedules, which are no more than the best executions of a strategy that is accepted by rote.

Chasing the Second Hare: Retail Research

During the mid-1980s, the focus of single-source research began to change sharply. The technique began to be used increasingly to measure short-term sales effects, but the concentration was on the sales effects of promotions and other in-store activities, rather than advertising. The specific research method was the diluted single-source system, and what made this system practicable and indeed simple to use was that the data were collected in retail stores. It became possible to measure accurately the immediate sales from a whole range of specific promotional actions, including their effect on competitive brands. The research was able to trace, in consumer purchasing terms, where the extra business from successful promotions was coming from: from extra purchases by users of the promoted brand or from users of competitive brands that could be identified.

This represented a large advance on the earlier store auditing system, and I shall shortly illustrate this superiority with a couple of examples. Although it is intrinsically interesting and also valuable to measure the effects of promotions, that is not the focus of this book. I will exercise self-restraint in the extent of the ground I cover here, particularly since the published case study material may not show typical patterns. Indeed, the examples published after the various ARF conferences all deal with single brands: individual instances of single-source evaluation. Single cases like these may illustrate more general patterns, but it is certainly not possible on this basis to make confident generalizations about macro effects.

Every type of in-store activity can be studied with diluted single-source research, and the various ARF papers include examples of all of the following:

- Test marketing
- Brand segmentation (including the analysis of consumers' brand repertoires)

- Management of manufacturers' brand portfolios
- Retail distribution (including regional variations and analyses of sales in different in-store locations)
- Total promotional budgets (including analyses of regional variations)
- Different promotional activities, including the distribution of budgets between alternatives: coupons, in-store display, and retail advertising
- Price alternatives, including coupons.

I shall stay briefly with the last of the stimuli listed above, and the two cases I shall outline say something about the depth and subtlety of the evaluation techniques used to measure their effects.

Price Optimization

In 1989, a major brand in a large food category increased its wholesale list price by 10 percent. At the time, SAMI-Arbitron's SamScan was still in the business of measuring retail sales by scanner, and this service was used by a competitor in the same category as the major brand. This competitor, who was mainly involved in manufacturing store brands, wanted to know how to respond to the price increase by the major brand. On the basis of weekly SamScan data covering an eighteen-month period, a number of analyses were made of the price elasticity of the manufacturer's most important store brand and the cross-elasticities between its different flavors.

Price elasticity is a numerical estimate of the amount by which sales of a brand will fall as a result of a 1 percent increase in its price (and how much they will rise as a result of a 1 percent fall in price). Cross-elasticity measures the effect of price changes on related lines: in this case on alternative flavors of the brand. If the price of flavor A goes up by 1 percent, how much will the sales of B and C go up in response to the fall in the sales of A?

A price elasticity is essentially a measure of substitutability—in other words, competition. The 10 percent increase in the original brand was going to affect the store brand in all events. But it was now important to estimate the effect on sales of the store brand if its price were also increased in turn.

The total research program comprised three stages. First, the elasticities and cross-elasticities were computed. Second, a large number of alternative prices were hypothesized and their overall effects worked out flavor by flavor, and also incrementally, to determine the total effect on the brand. The third step was to establish differential—but optimal—price levels for each flavor.

Before the arrival of single-source data, it was very often possible to calculate a price elasticity. The analyst needed enough historical data on different price and sales relationships to calculate averages. But working out a series of interrelated elasticities for a brand's varieties was a different problem altogether. Calculating cross-elasticities was only possible if the analyst did two things: first, track longitudinally (i.e., over time) the consumer sales of each of the flavors, and second, use a number of geographical regions where price experiments could be carried out.

This sophisticated procedure could only be done with the right research tools. "Scanning data was an essential element of this analysis. Thanks to the power which resides in its microlevel measurements (individual stores, UPC, weekly data), it can uncover major opportunities."[12]

Marginal Effects of Alternative Promotions

My second example tells the story of a major manufacturer of household cleaners with a portfolio of three brands. Budgetary pressures were compelling the manufacturer to reduce its promotions, and the BehaviorScan database was used to analyze the relative effects of couponing and certain other promotional activities. The analysis was based on estimates of incremental volume produced by each type of promotion.

For Brand A, coupons added a marginal 2.2 share points. If couponing were abandoned, less than half this business would be absorbed by the manufacturer's other brands, B and C, and more than half would be lost to competitive brands. Trade merchandising added a little less to Brand A, about 2 share points, but if this were abandoned, more than half the lost business would go to Brands B and C. Trade merchandising was therefore the more appropriate activity to cut back.

Similar analyses were made in turn for Brands B and C. The conclusion was that the reductions in the promotional budget had to be made in different ways. Brands A and B had funds taken out of their trade merchandising, and C had money cut from its couponing budget.

Before single-source research became available, it would have been very difficult to track through the market the effects of changes as small as two percentage points of share. This was only possible with a mechanism to trace in detail—purchase by purchase—how much of each brand was bought by individual consumers in response to experimental reductions in specific marketing variables. This had to be based on a test in a limited geographical area.

As with the first example, it is scanner data that made this type of analysis possible. "Applications such as understanding cross-brand cannibalization and the long-term effects of different marketing strategies require an in-depth understanding of the dynamics of consumer switching and loyalty."[13]

Useful though this sort of research may be, I must reiterate the point that it shifted the attention of the market research profession away from the evaluation of advertising effects. The more uses that were found for diluted single-source data, the less attention was applied to the more difficult job of measuring advertising. There is an obvious and quite sharp trade-off between the two activities that is connected with the ease of evaluating the one and the difficulty of evaluating the other.

One of the most widely publicized features of the marketing business during the past fifteen years has been the shift of emphasis away from advertising toward trade and consumer promotions. Estimates made by Cox Communications showed that in 1978, 42 percent of combined advertising plus promotional dollars went to advertising, with 58 percent going into sales promotions. Virtually every year between 1978 and 1996, the advertising proportion has fallen slightly but inexorably; in 1996, 76 percent of aggregate expenditure went into promotions and only 24 percent into advertising. Since then the proportions have stabilized.

There are a number of reasons for this striking trend. But many analysts —myself included—believe that because the sales effects of promotions are relatively easy to measure by diluted single-source research, manufacturers have been increasingly inclined to put more money into promotions. To such manufacturers, sales forecasting appears to have become a simpler, more reliable process than formerly. They have not boosted their expenditure on advertising because its effects are much more difficult to evaluate, requiring as they do the pure type of single-source measurement.[14]

However, manufacturers who boost their promotional budgets seem blithely unaware that this action is likely to hurt the profitability of their brands, as well as cause other long-term damage.[15] The move of large amounts of money into promotions—with their hidden costs and dangers —does, however, emphasize very strongly the need to use single-source research to address the effects of the other really important ingredient in the marketing mix. This brings me to what the research business has achieved to date in using single-source research to study advertising.

A Return to Essentials: Measuring Advertising Effects

By the end of the 1980s, the amount of diluted single-source research had been increasing for a decade. By this time, studies like those described in this appendix—and many permutations and variations—were being carried out by virtually all major marketers in the United States. But the use of single-source research to examine advertising effectiveness was still not very advanced.

A limited amount of advertising evaluation was being carried out, although the inability of the research industry to use the pure single-source method put a natural limit on the value of what was done. Of the eighty-one conference papers published by the ARF between 1988 and 1991, eleven were based on case study material related to advertising. In my opinion these included only two types of study of any real interest, on the basis of their originality and the importance of their conclusions. These are described below.

Advertising's Contribution to the Marketing Mix

Three ARF papers, relating to three separate brands, presented data that tracked each brand's sales week by week over a year. Each author then attempted, with considerable statistical ingenuity, to evaluate the specific contribution made by every one of the main marketing stimuli.[16]

This evaluation was carried out by regression analysis, a technique discussed in Chapter 1, and one that had been practiced for years before single-source research was first used. Multiple regression is calculated from a large number of statistical observations relating to separate variables, such as specific factors influencing sales, which can then be individually isolated. Single-source research, even in its diluted form, has been able to generate more statistical information (e.g., from weekly readings and regional data) than was ever before possible. This provides excellent fodder for regression analysis.

The three studies discussed here deconstruct the week-by-week sales of each brand. They estimate the percentage of each week's sales that can be accounted for by variables such as trade promotions, coupons,

Table C.3

Relative Importance of Marketing Inputs

Proportion of sales as a result of	Percent
Brand equity	79
Trade effect	13
Coupons	2
Advertising: short-term effect only	6
Total sales	100

Source: The data refer to a year's sales of a food product in Chicago, measured by Nielsen. Andrew M. Tarshis, "Results of the Latest Single-Source Analysis" (paper presented at ARF Conference, June 1989), p. 132.

advertising, and the underlying strength of the brand equity. Each element is peeled away like an onion skin, to provide a remarkably lucid estimate of the individual effect of each of the main sales stimuli.

These week-by-week analyses are then aggregated for the complete year. There are naturally variations among the different cases in the influence of the individual marketing variables; we are looking at different brands. However, one point of commonality between the different studies is that the greatest single influence on a brand's sales is the base equity of the brand. This is a compound of consumers' satisfaction with the brand's functional performance, and the added values or psychological rewards that come from repeated use of the brand, and from the advertising campaign, working as mutual reinforcements. It is related to what I mean by a brand's internal momentum, although my concept has a greater element of change built into it. It leads to a long-term growth in profit and often also in sales.

One of these analyses, covering a year, is shown in Table C.3. The data in Table C.3 show the short-term influence of advertising to be small but significant. Based on data from general studies of advertising, it is very possible that advertising's contribution at the margin is profitable. It could conceivably be paying for itself here.[17] The whole analysis is tidy, comprehensible, and extremely valuable for the manufacturer of the brand in question. But we should remember that if the pure single-source method had been used in this case to examine advertising, the effect of the latter could have been measured without complex multivariate regression.

I must reemphasize the point that we have no proof that the individual cases published by the ARF are typical of the field of repeat-purchase packaged goods as a whole. I am concerned in this book with finding out how many advertising campaigns work and how many do not. This can be done only if we look at numbers of brands. Fortunately, among the ARF conference papers, there is a single collection of inter-related papers that review advertising effects. This collection describes an important and interesting series of pressure-testing experiments carried out by IRI.[18]

The Influence of Increased Advertising Weight

Pressure testing—experiments with temporarily elevated levels of advertising weight—is a marketing device that has been used for decades. There is anecdotal evidence that one of the leading gasoline marketers in the United States once spent its whole advertising budget for two years in carrying out tests of this type—with generally inconclusive results. Nevertheless, such tests have often succeeded in swinging the sales needle and, sometimes, also the profit needle.[19]

Until the publication of the IRI study, the advertising industry had never seen anything as impressive as a collection of 293 tests of increased advertising weight, all assembled in one place. This mass of data was made possible by the area-by-area character of IRI's scanner research.[20]

The most important conclusion from this mine of information was that 49 percent of the 293 tests of boosted pressure managed to generate a sales increase: a rise in sales averaging 23 percent. A positive effect was more common with a campaign change than without one. It was greater when the media reach was increased than when it was not. And it was larger when the category itself was increasing in size than when it was static.

IRI tracked forty-four of its tests to determine whether the original sales increase was maintained after the advertising expenditure had been cut back to more normal levels. The research found a clear long-term effect. Comparing campaigns of increased pressure with those of constant pressure, the heavy-up advertising had a prolonged effect, producing twice the quantity of incremental sales over three years than over one year. Most of the incremental sales came from increased purchase frequency rather than from higher penetration, and the campaigns achieved this by persuading irregular buyers to buy more often.

Not surprisingly, the largest relative increases came from small brands and the largest absolute increases from large ones. IRI also drew interesting conclusions about the relationship between advertising and promotions. Advertising weight tests work best where trade promotional activity is low but the amount of consumer couponing is high. Finally—and not unexpectedly—the research uncovered a deafening disharmony between the copytest scores for the different campaigns and those campaigns' sales results.[21]

I have already explained that my own investigation, which is concerned with brands whose advertising budgets do not change much from year to year, covers different ground from the IRI study. In effect, the two are complementary, and some of the conclusions from the IRI research and my own are mutually reinforcing. But pressure testing by its nature is aggressive; it is carried out with the intention of generating sales increases. This is not always true of ongoing campaigns, especially those for large brands. In most cases, the role of advertising for these is defensive. Advertising's success is not always—not even often—measured by increases in market share. It is more concerned with protecting the status quo, although it sometimes succeeds in increasing slightly the purchase frequency of existing users, thus boosting profits.

The research in this book nevertheless provides examples of ongoing campaigns that managed to increase brand shares, but it also gives instances of campaigns that succeeded in defending a brand's current position. My examples were discussed in Chapters 7 and 9.

The First Quarter-Century of Single-Source Research

A quarter-century is a long period in the world of market research. Despite the large number of single-source or at least scanner investigations that have been carried out in the United States during this time, there are gaps—opportunities for further important work. Here is a summary of the developments that have taken place in the past and some ideas about what needs to be done in the future.

1. Single-source was first invented as a means of measuring the short-term effect of advertising. McDonald's pioneer experiment in 1966, despite its limitations, employed the pure single-source method.
2. McDonald's original work stimulated considerable interest and much discussion, particularly in the United States, but very little further research was actually carried out until the mid-1970s.

3. The introduction of supermarket scanners transformed the situation. At last, diluted single-source research became a practical possibility. But little or no research employed the pure method.

4. As a consequence of the advertising industry's response to the media implications of McDonald's original work, single-source research was applied first to problems of media tactics, in particular to measuring the size of television audiences in order to obtain effective frequency.

5. A possible ill effect of chasing the hare of effective frequency is that it may have contributed, and may still be contributing to some extent, to the wasteful deployment of advertising budgets.

6. From the mid-1980s, researchers began to use scanner research to measure retail sales and consumer purchases (in effect, two sides of the same coin). Most of this research was soon being used to chase a second hare: the evaluation of various types of retail activity, notably promotions.

7. An unexpected and unfortunate side effect of the concentration on retail activity is that it has drawn manufacturers toward promotions, which are easy to evaluate and often demonstrate strong short-term results—although these are mostly unprofitable. Manufacturers have progressively lost interest in advertising, which is difficult to measure and is commonly associated with weak—although often profitable—short-term effects.

8. Single-source researchers have published little aggregated data on the effectiveness of either promotions or advertising. There have been many published examples of individual successes, but it is impossible to generalize from these. The IRI study of 293 advertising pressure tests is a notable exception. But despite its value, it represents an examination of a special case. Pressure test programs are relatively unusual for most brands, and they are getting rarer.[22]

9. There are no aggregated studies of the effectiveness of ongoing advertising campaigns that are exposed at constant weight. This is the particular concern of this book.

10. Once the research industry is able to measure successfully and routinely the short-term effects of advertising, the industry should then address the following interconnected problems:

- How quickly will it be possible to detect campaigns that are not working and switch funds to something more productive?
- How easily will we be able to construct a short-term advertising response function for a brand in order to establish a reliable level of effective frequency? Is single-exposure effectiveness the general pattern?
- Will we be able to find out the extent to which advertising and promotions work in cooperation with each other? Can they be planned to work synergistically or must they always conflict?
- How can we better understand advertising's long-term effect? How can we ensure that all campaigns that generate a short-term response will also produce a long-term one?
- How can we use data on advertising's long-term effect to determine accurately advertising's marginal profitability?
- Will we be able to concentrate on the effective campaigns, arrive at the optimal advertising budget for each, and calculate how best this should be deployed over time?

The research in this book can contribute to answering these questions.

Notes

ARF is the acronym for Advertising Research Foundation.

1. The date of introduction of the UPC is mentioned by Ronald L. Lunde, "Using Scanner Data: Folklore and Fact," *Addressing Day-to-Day Problems with Scanner Data* (ARF Conference, June 1991), p. 206.

2. IRI has a rather rudimentary system for locating the actual brands advertised, based on reports from agencies and from Arbitron. These are then related to household purchases. The system falls short of the Monitor Plus method used by A.C. Nielsen. Michael G. Pailas, "Promotions or Advertising? Identifying a Better Mix" (paper presented at ARF Conference, June 1991), p. 142.

3. Laurence N. Gold, "Introduction to the Workshop: A Proper Definition of Terms," *Fulfilling the Promise of Electronic Single-Source Data* (paper presented at ARF Conference, June 1989), p. 6.

4. *Effective Frequency: The Relationship Between Frequency and Advertising Effectiveness*, Michael J. Naples, ed., (New York: Association of National Advertisers, 1979).

5. Archa O. Knowlton, Ira J. Schloss, Hubert A. Zielske, Michael J. Naples, Robert J. Schreiber, Clark Schiller, Marvin Belkin, Joseph W. Ostrow, William V. Behrmann, Herbert E. Krugman, James Spaeth, Gabe Samuels, Albert C. Rohloff, Colin McDonald, William J. McKenna, and Gerald J. Eskin, *Effective Frequency: The State of the Art, Current Media Applications, Next Steps from ARF* (papers presented at ARF Conference, June 1982).

6. *New Insights into Single-Source Data* (papers presented at ARF Conference, July 1988); *Fulfilling the Promise of Electronic Single-Source Data* (papers presented at

ARF Conference, June 1989); *Behavioral Research and Single-Source Data* (papers presented at ARF Conference, June 1990); *Addressing Day-to-Day Marketing Problems with Scanner Data* (papers presented at ARF Conference, June 1991); *Breakthrough Marketplace Advertising Research for Bottom Line Results* (papers presented at ARF Conference, November 1991).

7. Gold, "Introduction to the Workshop," p. 6.

8. Roger Godbeer, "Single-Source—What the Future Holds: Present Limitations and Evolving Opportunities" (paper presented at ARF Conference, July 1988), pp. 85–92; Andrew M. Tarshis and Arlene Pitts, "Wand and Card Panels: Issues and Emerging Applications" (paper presented at ARF Conference, June 1990), pp. 49–85; Anna Fountas, "Applications from Arbitron's ScanAmerica Database" (paper presented at ARF Conference, June 1990), pp. 85–92.

9. Timothy Joyce, "Intermedia Values and Single Source" *Electronic Media and Research Technologies—XI* (paper presented at ARF Conference, December 1992), pp. 127–140.

10. Godbeer, "Single-Source—What the Future Holds," p. 90.

11. Stephen A. Douglas, "How to Measure How Much Frequency is Enough" (paper presented at ARF Conference, July 1988), p. 77.

12. Daniel Ray, "In Search of the Optimum Price: A Case Study" (paper presented at ARF Conference, June 1990), pp. 133–149.

13. Linda Boland, "Using Household Scanner Data to Evaluate Marketing Mix Alternatives" (paper presented at ARF Conference, June 1991), pp. 54–63.

14. Researchers who have made the same point include Alice K. Sylvester, "Single Source . . . Single Force" (paper presented at ARF Conference, June 1990), p. 39; Pailas, "Promotions or Advertising?" p. 148; Michael J. Naples, "Bringing Advertising's Bottom Line Effectiveness Research Out of the Closet" (paper presented at ARF Conference, November 1991), p. 10.

15. John Philip Jones, "The Double Jeopardy of Sales Promotions" *Harvard Business Review*, September–October 1990, pp. 145–152.

16. Marilyn Henninger and Edward Dittus, "Single-Source Data: A Means, Not an End" (paper presented at ARF Conference, June 1989), pp. 83–102; Andrew M. Tarshis, "Results of the Latest Single-Source Analysis" (paper presented at ARF Conference, June 1989), pp. 119–137; Gian M. Fulgoni, "Market Mix Modeling with Single-Source Scanner Data" (paper presented at ARF Conference, June 1990), pp. 163–174.

17. Jones, "Double Jeopardy of Sales Promotions."

18. Leonard M. Lodish, "Key Findings from the 'How Advertising Works' Study." ARF Conference, November 1991, pp. 35–51; Beth Lubetkin, "Additional Major Findings from the 'How Advertising Works' Study." ARF Conference, November 1991, pp. 35–51.

19. Jones, "Double Jeopardy of Sales Promotions."

20. Lodish, "Key Findings"; Lubetkin, "Additional Major Findings."

21. The failings of copytesting are discussed in John Philip Jones and Jan S. Slater, *What's in a Name? Advertising and the Concept of Brands*, 2nd ed. (Armonk, NY: M.E. Sharpe, 2003), pp. 136–162.

22. There is evidence of a decline in the popularity of advertising pressure tests. Alan L. Baldinger, "The State of Test Marketing: Results of an ARF Survey" (paper presented at ARF Conference, June 1990), p. 198.

—————— Appendix D ——————

The Calculation of Advertising Intensity

Chapter 7 describes advertising intensity as follows: It is represented by the brand's share of total advertising in its category (share of voice), divided by its share of market. This calculation produces an estimate of how many percentage points of advertising voice there are for each percentage point of a brand's market share. In this way, we can compare brands of different sizes according to their relative investment in advertising.

If we used share of voice on its own for the calculation, the big brands would automatically be given greater prominence than the small ones. This is the reason for going through the additional piece of arithmetic to calculate expenditure according to share of market.

Nielsen generates a very valuable measure of a brand's advertising exposure—the percentage of category purchase occasions preceded by advertisements for each brand during the preceding seven days. The figures are presented quarterly, and nearly all brands covered by this research were advertised over all four quarters of 1991. These figures formed the basis of my calculation of advertising intensity. I arrived at the estimate for each brand by going through the following three steps, which are illustrated by the data from the bar soaps category in Table D.1.

1. I averaged the figures for the quarterly purchases preceded by advertising exposure, and I aggregated the total for the category.

Table D.1

Advertising Intensity Calculation: Bar Soaps Category

Brand	Category purchase occasions preceded by ads (percent)	Share of voice (percent)	Share of market, first-quarter 1991 (percent)	Advertising intensity
CA	20.6	8	15.7	0.5
CB	28.6	11	13.3	0.8
CC	12.7	5	10.4	0.5
CD	25.2	10	5.0	2.0
CE	34.8	14	8.2	1.7
CF	27.8	11	7.1	1.5
CG	11.0	4	5.6	0.7
CH	24.6	10	4.2	2.4
CJ	20.1	8	3.8	2.1
CK	—	—	2.6	—
CL	—	—	0.6	—
CM	—	—	3.1	—
CN	21.9	9	1.0	9.0
CO	7.1	3	3.0	1.0
All others	17.8	7	16.6	0.4
Total		100	100.0	

This represents the gross duplicated volume of purchases preceded by advertising.

2. On the basis of this total, I calculated each brand's share of voice by simple percentaging. (Strictly speaking, each share represents the brand's share of purchases preceded by advertising. This is a sensitive and precise, although unorthodox, measure of share of voice.)

3. By dividing each brand's market share (first quarter 1991) into its share of voice, I calculated its percentage points of advertising voice for each percentage point of market share. The result is the brand's advertising intensity.

It is interesting to compare the calculations of share of voice in Table D.1 with estimates derived from the independent media measurement organization Leading National Advertisers (LNA). The two sets of data appear in Table D.2.

Two points emerge from the comparison of the two research systems.

The first point is that the All Others group is much larger in the LNA tabulation. One reason is that the smaller brands that constitute the All

Table D.2

Comparison of Shares of Voice: Nielsen and LNA (in percent)

Brand	Nielsen	LNA
CA	8	7
CB	11	10
CC	5	5
CD	10	13
CE	14	7
CF	11	5
CG	4	included in all others
CH	10	6
CJ	8	7
CK	—	—
CL	—	—
CM	—	—
CN	9	9
CO	3	included in all others
All others	7	31
Total	100	100

Others group use print media more than the named brands do. Print media are audited by LNA but not by Nielsen. Another reason for the difference is that my research is based on special tabulations of Nielsen data. Brands down to 1 or 2 percent market share were individually tabulated, and less attention was paid individually to the tiny brands that are in the All Others group. The advertising information for these was therefore probably undercounted. This makes no difference at all to the analyses in this book, since my concern throughout is with comparisons between identified brands. Absolute levels of advertising expenditure are not therefore important.

The second point is that for CD, the LNA figure is larger; for CE, CF, and CH, the Nielsen figures are higher than the LNA ones. These four brands make an interesting comparison. The Nielsen figures relate to buyers' exposure to a brand's advertising (which is why they are used as the basis for the advertising intensity estimates in this book). The LNA figures are based on objective estimates of financial outlay on media space and time. The fact that, for any brands, the Nielsen figures are higher than the LNA ones means that the media targeting of users was very effective for those brands. This is true for CE, CF, and CH. For CD, however, the opposite holds. These examples show that the tactical efficiency of media buying is relevant to the long-term progress of brands.

—— Appendix E ——

The Leading 142 Brands in the Product Categories Covered in This Research

Packaged Detergents

All, Arm & Hammer, Bold, Cheer, Dash, Fab, Oxydol (with Bleach), Purex, Surf, Tide, Tide (with Bleach), Wisk (with Power Scoop)

Liquid Detergents

Ajax, All, All (Free Clear), Arm & Hammer, Cheer, Cheer (Free), Dash, Era, Purex, Solo, Surf, Tide, Wisk, Wisk (Advanced Action), Yes, store brands

Bar Soaps

Camay, Caress, Coast, Dial, Dove, Irish Spring, Ivory, Jergens Mild, Lever 2000, Pure & Natural, Safeguard, Shield, Tone, Zest

Shampoos

Alberto VO5, Breck, Finesse, Head & Shoulders, Ivory, Pert Plus, Rave, Revlon Flex, Salon Selectives, Style, Suave, Vidal Sassoon, White Rain, store brands

Toilet Tissue

Angel Soft, Charmin, Coronet, Cottonelle, Kleenex, Nice 'n Soft, Northern, Scottissue, Soft 'n Gentle, White Cloud, store brands

Ice Cream

Blue Bell, Borden, Breyers, Dreyer's Grand/Edy's Grand, Kemps, Meadow Gold, Quality Chekd, Sealtest, Turkey Hill, Well's Blue Bunny, store brands

Mayonnaise

Blue Plate, Duke's, Hellmann's/Best Foods, Hellmann's (Light), JFG, Kraft, Weight Watchers, store brands

Peanut Butter

Adams, Jif, Laura Scudders, Peter Pan, Simply Jif, Skippy, Smucker's, store brands, generics

Ground Coffee

Chase & Sanborn, Chock Full o' Nuts, Eight O'Clock, Folger's, High Yield, Hills Bros., Master Blend, Maxwell House, MJB, Yuban, store brands

Diet Carbonated Soft Drinks

A & W, Coca-Cola, Coca-Cola (Caffeine Free), Diet Rite (Caffeine Free), Dr. Pepper, Mountain Dew, Pepsi-Cola, Pepsi-Cola (Caffeine Free), Seven Up, Shasta, Sprite

Breakfast Cereals

General Mills Apple Cinnamon Cheerios, General Mills Cheerios, General Mills Honey Nut Cheerios, General Mills Lucky Charms, General Mills Wheaties, Kellogg's Corn Flakes, Kellogg's Frosted Flakes, Kellogg's Frosted Mini-Wheats, Kellogg's Fruit Loops, Kellogg's Raisin Bran, Kellogg's Rice Krispies, Post Grape Nuts, Post Premium Raisin Bran, store brands

Analgesics

Advil, Anacin, Bayer, Excedrin, Good Health, Motrin IB, Nuprin, Tylenol, Your Life, store brands, generics

Index

About the Author

John Philip Jones is a specialist in the measurement and evaluation of advertising effects and the originator of two widely used concepts to measure them. He was educated as an economist, with bachelor's and master's degrees from Cambridge University. He worked as a market researcher and manager of advertising accounts in Europe for twenty-seven years, twenty-five of them with the J. Walter Thompson Company, where he focused on the effects of advertising. He has spent twenty-five years at the Newhouse School of Public Communications, Syracuse University, where he is a tenured full professor. He is a visiting professor at the Copenhagen Business School, Denmark, and has served as an adjunct professor at the Royal Melbourne Institute of Technology, Australia.

He travels all over the world as a consultant for many first-rank national and international organizations, mainly advertisers and advertising agencies.

He is the author of more than seventy articles and the editor and co-author of a series of five handbooks on advertising practice, representing the largest single collection of professional and academic papers written on the subject (1998–2000). He has written seven books, including *When Ads Work*, first edition (1995), *The Ultimate Secrets of Advertising* (2001), *Fables, Fashions and Facts About Advertising*: *A Study of 28 Enduring Myths* (2003), and *How to Turn Advertising Expenses into Investments* (2005). His books have been translated into nine foreign languages.

John Philip Jones has received a number of national awards from the American Advertising Federation and other bodies. In 2001 he received the Syracuse University Chancellor's Citation for Exceptional Academic Achievement. In 2003 he was nominated, by the journal *American Demographics*, as one of the "25 most influential people on the demographic landscape over the past two-and-a-half decades."